THE ECONOMICS OF CONVULSION

A Japan-U.S. Affair

Harold E. Wills
Charles Walters Jr.

THE ECONOMICS OF CONVULSION

A Japan-U.S. Affair

Harold E. Wills
Charles Walters Jr.

Acres U.S.A.
Kansas City, Missouri

The Economics of Convulsion

Acres U.S.A., Publishers
Box 9547, Kansas City, Missouri 64133-9547

ISBN: 0-911311-34-3
Library of Congress Card Catalog: 91-077482

Dedicated to the
memory of the late
Arnold E. Paulson,
National Organization of Raw Materials'
greatest spokesman

ABOUT THE AUTHORS

Harold E. Wills was born in Detroit, Michigan, but spent his childhood in Hutchinson, Kansas, where his great-grandparents had been among the first settlers. After service in the Army Air Corps he attended Washington University, St. Louis, Missouri, while working nights as a beat reporter for the now-defunct *Globe-Democrat*. After graduation, he was assigned to the Washington Bureau of this newspaper. Since then, he has covered the world, representing such as the old International News Service, *Newsweek*, United Press and Tropical New Service. When the regional cooperative FAR-MAR-CO was formed, he was asked to become its director of communications and Washington liaison, a position he held until 1973 when Kansas Governor Robert Docking asked him to create and head a state energy office able to cope with the OPEC oil embargo. Also, he represented Kansas in Washington during this period. After leaving this post, he was appointed by the Sedgwick County Court to become operating receiver of a nationwide trucking company with global business. A year later, this was merged into a global carrier and the assignment ended. The same year, he became part of a twelve-person crew under contract the the International Trade Administration and charged with opening new markets for the U.S. on a global basis. This was the last aggressive move made by the U.S., and it was dismantled after only two years in the field. Since then, Wills has spent his time in writing, and in serving as advisor to several national financial institutions, operating from an office in downtown Hutchinson. He is also a special reporter for *Acres U.S.A.*

Charles Walters Jr. was born in Ness County, Kansas in 1926. A veteran of WWII and the Korean activity, he holds a bachelor's degree from Creighton University, Omaha, and a graduate degree in economics from the University of Denver. He is a former publisher's assistant for *Veterinary Medicine* magazine, and more recently founder and publisher of *Acres U.S.A.* He is well known for his works on agriculture, and is author of *Holding Action* (1968), *Angry Testament* (1969), *Unforgiven* (1971), *The Case for Eco-Agriculture* (1975), *An Acres U.S.A. Primer* (1979), *Weeds, Control Without Poisons* (1990), *Raw Materials Economics* (1991), and *The Economics of Convulsion* with Harold E. Wills (1992). He is also editor of *The Albrecht Papers* (1975), *The Carbon Connection* (1990) and *Mainline Farming For Century 21* (1991). His biography, *A Life in the Day of An Editor* (1986) is the story of the newspaper he edits, *Acres U.S.A.* His book, *Parity, The Key to Prosperity Unlimited* (1982), is considered definitive in the field. He is also author of many articles on farm technology.

Table of Contents

Bankruptcy is not merely a moral device or a way to achieve equity, it is primarily the especial condition for the efficiency of the price mechanism of the economic system which is usually called capitalism. The system would collapse without it, deprived of the sole compulsion which obliges the individual to bring his otherwise unimpeded activities into conformity with the conditions necessary for the survival of the system.—*Jacques Reuff, writing in* The Age of Inflation, *1948*

FOREWORD

THE LAND IS THE SOURCE of everything in every nation and has a value that is unchanging, dictated by its presence and its productivity. From the dawn of history, this has been the cornerstone of all studies of economics and the cause of more wars than any political ideology devised by mankind. It was the driving force behind the creation of vast empires by Rome, Greece, England, Spain and other nations gone from the mind and memory of man.

The promise of wealth in the form of land triggered the settlement of the U.S. west of the Appalachians, across the Great Plains and onward to the Pacific coastline. Once the land was settled, and immediate value was created, this later could be converted into cash and monetized via the mechanism of production times price. The land and its production drove the value of the currency rather than the opposite.

Every nation throughout history that has sought to reverse this basic rule has crumbled and fallen. Every nation, with the exception of the tiny trading entities such as Monaco, that has sought to substitute currency for the wealth represented by land and its raw materials value, has fallen and vanished. The same has been true for every nation which has divorced its interpretation of wealth from the land and its produce, substituting paper digits that could be exchanged internally like trading stamps, but which could not be permitted to enter the international arena of true currencies. The latest victim of this charade has been Soviet Russia, where the ruble had value only as an internal method of exchange, but which was worthless in the world market despite the vast land area of the USSR. This scheme was a deliberate prostitution of the laws of currencies, and it failed.

Japan, by monetizing its land at artificial, astronomical values and expanding this process to include Japanese-owned land in South America, within the United States, in Mexico and elsewhere, is violating every natural rule and is courting disaster. It has monetized its land so high, in theory, that tiny nation of islands could buy up the world. Some of its Tokyo acres, up to six inches deep, are worth more than the present price of gold. A collapse of its real estate values in the same degree the Nikkei Dow has fallen—48% between the last quarter of 1989 and the third quarter of 1990—would be equal to reducing the entire world's stock markets to zero. The loss on the Nikkei—if real estate followed—might be calculated at $8 trillion U.S.

Japan's population is obeying the Malthusian equation, expanding every day. Much of everything eaten, worn and used must be imported from elsewhere in the world. Without conquest of some other land-mass adequate to become a supply source, Japan is incapable of meeting its domestic demands. But, it has devised a temporary solution. It has monetized its holdings the world over by acquiring overseas assets and capturing the marketplaces of nations where true wealth still exists.

This includes the United States but, in our case, it could spell disaster for both participants. The U.S. is blindly following a variation of the same theme. For more than two decades, blinded by our temporary success, we have been monetizing electronic digits and federal flim-flam that revolves around creative mathematics that convert basic economics into a revolving door. Our government, our university system, our markets and our daily domestic commerce are snared in this scheme from which escape is impossible without triggering a mounting disaster.

Our land is papered with a veneer of debt that is beyond any hope of translation by basic mathematics. Our domestic and international commerce is governed by electronic money and currency that does not exist. Our federal deficit, created to support this monstrosity, is beyond hope of erasure or even reversal. We are on a treadmill from which the only escape is economic disaster. One spark is all that is needed to launch an irreversible erasure.

It could be said that the U.S., from innocence or arrogance, is following in the footsteps of other powers of the past which have fallen by spending their future, but this would not, for the U.S., be true. In the crucible of World War II and its aftermath, we became a dynamo of exciting new knowledge and swept the world along on our coattails. We created a new Japan from radioactive shambles and we led in creation of a new level of global civilization based upon our new knowledge penetrating new areas never before explored in the classroom or the laboratory.

But, somehow, as the years passed and others acquired our new knowledge, we became defensive and retreated into the comfortable familiarity of a vanished past, which was simple enough to be understood.

This attitude penetrated our university system which, instead of leading government, became captive to it in a blind reliance upon every scrap of official data that would become the benchmarks of learning. Three generations of graduates conduct their lives on the basis of these official data which, as we now know, are often flawed because the root from which they sprouted was flawed.

This is especially true in the multi-level fields of economics, where failed policies of the past—whitewashed in the passage of years—have been grafted upon new packages infested with comfortable buzz-words from the past and then foisted upon the nation and the world. Our thinkers are wrapped within a cocoon of these flawed instruments, and today this is becoming painfully visible. Things just don't work as they should. The results of a shining new policy package are the opposite of what was intended and supported by a host of comfortable buzz-words and references.

This charade happened once before in history, in France, at a time when image was more important than substance and when the national wealth was squandered until nothing was left but the image itself and the nation was bankrupt, its government fallen and replaced by civil chaos. Today, the first signs of this blind parade toward disintegration are visible within the economic society of the United States. But, like France in that bygone day, image continues to have priority over provable substance and historical parallels are ignored and are not even a part of university learning.

France marched to its pivot point with majesty. The U.S. is just romping blindly down the same pathway, stubbornly clinging to familiar axioms with no thought of the ultimate consequences, or of alternate avenues based upon solid, provable facts that have been tucked away within a stored and abandoned computer tape, or as reams of paper buried somewhere within a dusty warehouse, location forgotten.

The following chapters penetrate these old warehouses and the forgotten computer tapes and draw upon the past to illustrate the present and the *Catch-22* dilemma into which we are moving ourselves in our national innocence and stubborn blindness. Step by step, the march toward our coming day of reckoning is outlined in stark detail and, as examples of the ultimate and inevitable conclusion, parallels from other nations are included. Are we, as seems likely, approaching our national economic crossroads where the wrong final decision can guarantee oblivion? Is it already too late? Will most of our population—as in Argentina after the age-old laws of economics were scrapped—live in poverty by the end of this century?

By the time answers to these questions are known, it may be too late for reversal and renewal. It may already be too late. After reading the following chapters, you must be the judge. Enroute, keep in mind the words of Evita Peron as she left her native land, "Don't cry for me, Argentina. Cry for yourself."

—1—

THE GOD EMPEROR

COINAGE IS THE POLITICS of scarcity. It is only a mathematical tool used to create competition and establish a measurable value based upon scarcity. Even though it is only a base mineral with little useful value, gold was used for centuries as a medium of exchange because it was scarce. Realistically, anything—gold, silver, chicken feathers, thin air—could have been used as a basis for value—as long as it was controlled, blessed with currency status and flexible.

This reasoning was the starting point for the team assembled by General Douglas MacArthur at the close of World War II, and charged with the task of rebuilding Japan into a competitive democratic power. The team began its efforts with the equivalent of a blank sheet of paper because Japan was in a state of collapse, wrung dry by the decade-long war that had begun with the invasion of Manchuria, and expanded throughout the Pacific Ocean following a surprise attack upon Pearl Harbor on December 7, 1941. When the war ended, Japan was only a hollow shell with more than a thousand years of tradition destroyed.

For half a century, Japan had seized property in Asia because modernization required raw materials. After his rise to the chrysanthemum thorne, Hirohito approved Japan's seizure of a New England-sized piece of Manchuria in 1931, the Kansas-sized province of Jehol in 1933, and Montana-sized Inner Mongolia in 1935. In 1937 Japan launched a full-scale invasion of all that was left of China—from the Great Wall in the north to the borders of Indochina, Thailand, Burma and India in the south, all under the direction of a leader who kept himself informed on military matters down to the regimental level and who actively directed strategy and planning for WWII. This humble old man ordered two hundred thousand Chinese executed at Nanking, five thousand girls and women raped and killed, Chinese soldiers split from pate to groin with a single stroke of the Samurai sword. He ordered the Pearl Harbor plan drawn up six months before Tojo heard of it, and he then ordered it executed. The Panay was sunk into Yangtze River mud on his orders, and half of the Allied prisoners died due to mistreatment—on the Bataan death march, taking the bridge and railroad over the river Kwai, in stinking mines and in death camps, where unspeakable medical experiments annhilated men by the hundreds and thousands—all because the god emperor wanted it, ordered it.

And when it was all over a Peace Faction was manufactured, credentialed with suitable arrest records, and set into office to rule by U.S. occupation forces. The emperor at that time said the throne might have to wait one hundred years to reclaim its heritage.

Somehow, in the years of occupation government that followed, American history failed to recognize or identify the most important factor in the rebuilding of Japan into a new Western-oriented society.

Never before in three thousand years of recorded history has a nation been manufactured so quickly on the basis of rational, scientific reasoning. Before and after 1945, every nation since the dawn of civilization has been a product of evolution with abrupt directional changes reflecting the whims of the leader in power at any moment. Each fallen empire of the past left a trail of ruinous mistakes as part of the testament to its existence. The United States, in its brief existence, contributed to this panorama but provided a handy measurement baseline for two reasons. It was the victor in the war just ended. And, it had a fetish for record keeping that included even the most insignificant facts.

In construction of a new economic and geographical society in Japan, an intense scrutiny of the global past became a key element. The nation was unique in several respects. It was a relative newcomer on the world stage because, for many centuries, Japan had existed in hidden isolation. It lacked almost every natural resource needed for a nation's survival as an independent power. Its society was a mix of mysticism and ambition that was unfocused. And, its government was a hybrid combining religion with a hodge-podge of knowledge acquired from Japan's historically brief role on the world stage.

Every level of Japanese society was accustomed to bowing to higher authority and this was a major asset for the MacArthur team in its creation of a new "manufactured" nation occupying a land area too small and too unproductive to support the population expansion that was inevitable. Because it is the basis of all transactions, the team's work began with the Japanese currency.

Apparently because of tradition and for no other reason, the currency of nations has been based directly or indirectly upon their stocks of gold. The United States, a newcomer on the world stage, enjoyed quick wealth because its land was blessed with apparently endless gold deposits. Printing of the U.S. dollar could be expanded apparently endlessly as long as gold was grubbed from the earth in the western states and territories. With an apparently inexhaustible supply of this mineral, living standards in the U.S. could be ratcheted upward with each generation and the central government in Washington could remain debt-free despite the series of wars fought with various powers. Not clearly understood was the fact that the physical economy had the function of making good every expansion of the money supply.

Japan had none of these advantages. Its mountains contained no big gold deposits. Only a small portion of each island was suitable for growing crops or raising livestock. Its industrial base was a shambles, either very primitive or razed by American bombs during the final months of the war. Raw materials for the existence of new factories had to be imported from somewhere else in the world, thus making Japan vulnerable to political decisions or conflicts within these other lands. Worst of all, Japan consisted of a series of small islands that, in theory, were incapable of supporting even a token population.

These were the obstructions faced by the MacArthur team as it groped to develop a formula to permit Japan to survive, prosper and become an acceptable member of the world community of nations. In their search for a basis for Japan's new currency, the team eliminated all possibilities but one—the land itself. Why not the land? After all, coinage is the politics of scarcity and when Japan's growing population was included in the calculations—there was nothing more scarce than land upon which the Japanese of the future would live!

Thus, the land itself was monetized. It became the baseline value for the currency, a baseline that in theory could be cranked up or down as needed to guarantee a constantly rising level of affluence for the Japanese people. But, to be truly workable on the global stage, the newly stabilized currency had to be accompanied by a steadily rising volume of industrial production on two levels.

One was production to be consumed by the rest of the world, thus creating a subsidy for the inputs that would need to be imported to keep the Japanese factories in operation. The other level was production for consumption within Japan, but partially subsidized by the global trade. To accomplish these goals, an entirely new form of corporate society had to be invented. The result was a curious mix between the traditional stockholder-owned corporations of the West, and the somewhat mystical background of Japanese businesses. The corporations would be stockholder-owned in the fashion of the United States, Great Britain and Germany and traded on a stock exchange to be created—but with token holdings owned by the central government, whose duty would be to keep things humming for the national good, avoiding harmful corporate conflicts of the type common in the West. The central government, with the emperor as its figurehead, would direct production for the common good of the entire nation. Favoritism was avoided because the central government collected from everybody on the basis of profit!

With the currency (the yen) stabilized by the decision to peg its value to the land, the next step was integration of the banking system into those involving currency and production. It was the duty of the bankers to provide funds downward to the consumers, and upward to the new industries that would be created. The bankers were more than cooperative for two reasons. The newly-revamped currency was being stabilized into acceptance throughout the world. And, second, with the Emperor as a silent partner in their operations, the new industries posed no credit risk.

Piece by piece, the MacArthur team sifted through the entire economic fabric of Japan, "manufacturing" a new nation unlike anything that had existed before throughout recorded history. Once the Japanese people saw the direction things were headed, and examined the first physical results, they were extremely cooperative—even though they remained ignorant of the grand design. Everybody had a job. Living standards were rising steadily, and for the first time in history, plenty of sound and solid money was circulating through the land.

Top priorities were given to education and innovation; compulsory schooling became a standard part of Japanese life. Children learned to be proud of being Japanese and they learned to be ambitious. The attitude implanted in these children was global, not confined solely to Japan. This was deliberate because one of the first things learned by the MacArthur team was that Japan could not survive in isolation. As a nation, she could not feed or support herself. The MacArthur team was preparing Japan for the future—not the present. Time, for this team, was short. They would leave as soon as Japan was able to support herself and thrive from the new direction they had created.

Agriculture also received attention from the Americans who were manufacturing a nation. As an independent entity able to feed the growing population, it was hopeless. This has been true for several centuries and was the reason why Japan depended increasingly upon the oceans for its food. Without daily access to the sea by its commercial fishing fleets, Japan would starve. But, a trickle of foodstuffs came from the small farms in the arable valleys of the Japanese islands. The Americans concentrated their attention upon these farms.

With a portion of the profits from factories going automatically into the national treasury, money would not be a problem once the factory output penetrated the world marketplace. Part of the team favored using some of these funds to provide a subsidy to the farmers. The others preferred legal imposition of floor prices to guarantee profits to agriculture. In the end, both won. Prices were pegged above the cost of production, and certain crops were given subsidies. Importation of foodstuffs was assigned to the industrial sector because its future would be global—that is, not restricted to the Japanese mainland.

As a guarantee against future shortages of foodstuffs, a scheme termed "plantation outreach" was created, to be activated after Japan had become established in the world marketplace, and its population density was approaching the critical point where, without constant imports of food, mass hunger would erupt within a matter of weeks. This critical point was forecast to appear about the year 1978.

The plantation outreach program was adopted from British history during the reign of Queen Victoria and was adapted to fit Japanese circumstances as a power emerging from defeat in the most deadly war in the history of mankind.

Victorian England lived in opulence because plantations were scattered around the world in colonial possessions conquered by Great Britain and added to its empire. These plantations existed for two reasons. One, of course, was to earn a trade profit because of the low wages paid to the native laborers. The other mandate was to ship part of each year's crop back to England to maintain its prosperity. Indirectly, this scheme was one of the causes of the American Revolution.

Japan had lost any desire for conquest or creation of a colonial empire. Also, a colonial empire was forbidden by the American conquerors. But, mercantile conquest was not. In fact, it was encouraged as a way to make Japan more prosperous. The resulting master plan included a "population trigger," a point in the future when the population density in the home islands became so great that Japan would become dependent upon imported foodstuffs for its national survival. When that point was reached, land would be acquired by purchase in developing nations around the world, and crops would be grown on this land for shipment to Japan. Deliberately, land purchases would be scattered, and in a variety of nations, so that if one acquired a hostile new government, the others would remain intact. By this means, a steady stream of foodstuffs would be assured.

Because these overseas plantations would be operated by Japanese managers and executive assistants, they would provide new opportunities for the graduates of Japanese universities. Transportation to and from the installations would be, of course, provided by Japanese vessels and aircraft. Development of these agricultural colonies would be keyed to population growth within the home islands. Every tool and machine used on these plantations would be manufactured in Japanese factories, thus stimulating industrial output on a captive basis. Exposure of these machines to the natives of other lands would be a form of advertising for Japanese products and would be followed by Japanese salesmen offering attractive financing plans to potential buyers.

This was the "plantation outreach" plan to be activated when Japan's population was approaching the trigger point. It was a key element in the manufacture of a new global power. The MacArthur team was unique in history because it faced absolutely no restrictions imposed for bureaucratic reasons. It could requisition whatever it needed—and that included personnel and ideas. Part of the staff assembled in Tokyo did nothing but search for ideas that might be adapted to the manufacturing of a new nation. A concept that might be outlandish in the United States could solve a problem in Japan. It was not unusual for an American with a publicized idea to be summoned to Tokyo for an audience with MacArthur's "think tank" personnel.

No Keynesian, MacArthur nevertheless asked for and got $2 billion in economic aid from Washington. More important, MacArthur's team drew a lesson from Toberius Semponius Gracchus (163-133 B.C.), who gave the land back to small independent growers. Operating out of a rickety annex of the Dai Ichi, Brigadier General William Marquat—with teams too numerous to mention—kept red flags from appearing in the Japanese countryside. Later it was observed that MacArthur—who wanted to solve the issue of communism on the battlefield—was most successful in preempting the issue that took Mao Tse-tung to power and Marshall's China hands into oblivion at the end of WWII. That issue was land reform.

—2—

THE DREAMS OF AVARICE

NEVER IN HISTORY HAD A NATION been so completely beaten, with perhaps the exception of China. And at the end of WWII, two military giants were handed the task of solving both "impossibles." George C. Marshall went to China. Douglas MacArthur was made a veritable dictator in Japan. The outline that emerged from MacArthur's think tanks proceeded to face down the reality that had always destroyed reconstruction efforts in the past—harshness of policy and inflation.

When Harry S Truman sent Marshall to China, the specter of hunger, destruction and internecine strife loomed large on the horizon. War Lords were still operative or in loose alliance with Chiang Kai-shek, and Mao Tse-tung's communists were making their bid to take over all the country. Inflation was running rampant. In China as elsewhere in history, the course of inflation—economical, political and moral—had followed the same pattern.

By 1947, CNC 11 million (CNC meaning Chinese National Currency) had some value during the last week of December that year. It was still worth about $100 American. The official exchange rate was CNC 12,000 to $1, a nominal and quite meaningless figure. As Franz Pick would be quick to point out, official exchange is rot. What does the real market—the black market—have to say? At the end of 1947, the black market exchange rate was CNC 150,000 to 1. By the start of 1948 it was CNC 200,000 to 1. By mid-March it was CNC 500,000 to 1. Nothing like it had happened in civilized society since the German inflation post-WWI. The chaos this created had run beyond instant comprehension. A businessman might sell something for CNC 50,000. A month later, when he collected, his money was worth 33% less. A worker earning the equivalent of $10 a month would find his pay cut to the value of $2 a month in 60 days. A housewife would go into a shop for rice. In the hour it took to shop, some CNC 100,000 would be added to the price. Rice riots became the inevitable result—not so much because of shortage, but because shop operators closed early so they could sell inventory at tomorrow's higher prices. By 1948, CNC notes weren't worth as much as the cost of the paper it took to print them. The government responded in the usual way, by printing higher denominations.

While the people suffered, officials and the powers that be quickly turned CNC notes into American currency or gold bars. For these fortunate few, inflation paved the road to wealth beyond the dreams of avarice. Travelers returning from China during those days told about the other side of the equation. Common people were forced to spend their money before the sun went down. By tomorrow it wouldn't buy as much.

Chiang relied on a lot of experts, both Chinese and American, General George C. Marshall included. Just as American schools were starting classes in the fall of 1948, Chiang came out with his ill-fated and belated currency reform. This proved to be the straw that broke the back of the middle class. The Gold Yuan replaced the CNC. The same announcement ordered the turning in of all foreign currency, gold, silver and precious objects, because the GY was to equal stability plus.

GYs were printed in the U.S. They had an exchange rate of GY 4 to 1 American.

Chiang Ching-kuo, the son of Chiang Kai-shek, was named economic tsar of Shanghai, China's financial center. The public prints told about arrests of "bigs" and street executions of "not-so-bigs." From vantage point U.S.A., it looked as if the authorities meant business. But it was too late, and the gold the United States provided was simply stolen by Chiang Kai-shek's henchmen.

The outcome of all this suggests a riddle first posed a few decades ago, but which has become more haunting by the hour: are we looking at history, or are we looking at prophecy? The printing press has always been the last resort of the rascal prince. As the world screams for help, as the crazies in government sink deeper in debt, history's dictum comes home. *Those who know no history are condemned to repeat it.* Thus our interest in the super cycles of history, hyper-inflation, and the upcoming convulsion scenario being structured by public policy. That convulsion will likely proceed as deflation first, then hyper-inflation as officials reach for a quick fix. At issue is the question whether Japan's experience will excuse it from what appears to be a world-wide convulsion.

These several observations have prompted an in-depth look at Bresciana-Tourroni's *The Economics of Inflation.* Bresciani-Tourroni wrote in staccato sentences. His opening chapters were as hammer sharp as the events that led to the German wheelbarrow inflation of the early 1920s. For instance, a loaf of bread cost 428,000,000 marks in November of 1923. A year earlier, the entire equity capitalization of the Daimler Corporation could have been purchased for the equivalent cost of three hundred twenty-seven of its cars. And that is what is meant by *wheelbarrow inflation*.

Inflation is always a monetary phenomenon. All other explanations are just so much pragmatic meaninglessness. By this we mean inflation is and means inflation of money and credit. The fact that prices rise is an *effect*, not a *cause*.

In the late teens and the early 1920s, Germany endured an inflation because of war finance, loss of territories, and reparations. The trigger mechanism for the German fiasco surfaced and soured when gold convertibility was suspended. This enabled the central banking structure to discount notes with a governing device. At the end of WWI, the socialist regime did not have the will or the power to raise taxes, or to operate a balanced budget, or to seek a structural balance for the economy. Being a socialist government, it presumed to keep the worst effects of unemployment from showing up by institutionalizing poverty, and by turning parasite people into bureaucrats and counselors of state.

Only the least literate will fail to see how closely these things parallel post WWII conditions in the U.S. First, the U.S. endured war finance, and then it paid out reparations. These reparations took the form of Marshall Plan money, which financed loincloth production in Africa and the South Seas, production having to do with common denominator raw materials such as fats and oils. Sharp international bankers sold, and dull Congressmen bought, the commie-under-every-rock thesis, and this prompted the nation to pour its reparations to the far corners of the world so free trade could rupture American solvency. All might have been handled had the nation preserved its price structure with legislation. In fact, however, lawmakers who were and remain ignorant of economic laws agreed that American farmers should sell at world prices. Reparations made it possible for foreigners to compete, and devaluation by the British and the sterling bloc nations caused the U.S. to become the world's high market. As goods poured in, farm income sank. National economic profits fell below a maintenance level. This opened debt creation. After 1950, each decade was to see the doubling and redoubling of the public and private debt. Accordingly, the countryside emptied—60% of the farm operators posting their "having decided to quit farming" notices in short order. The government program count passed the count of the 1930s as socialized regime after regime sought to avoid taxation and expanded the money supply to accommodate a steady rate of inflation. Except for in-depth students, this form of chain letter economics did not rate attention until the U.S. suspended gold convertibility—de facto in 1968, de jure in 1971.

The substitute-debt-for-earnings theme really got a toehold when farm parity slid in the early Eisenhower years. By the time Kennedy took office, campaign rhetoric called for the nation to get moving again. The New Economists were assuring the young president that a little inflation was good for the system. They did not tell him that a "little inflation" was like the potion Circe gave the shipwrecked sailors who happened on her isle, a drug that turned men into swine. They did not tell him that the end results would be a system so illiquid that the process could not be reversed without convulsion.

Bank Credit Analyst correctly pointed to the fact that once liquidity is run down below a critical stage, "a self-feeding illiquidity/inflation spiral is unleashed that no one in authority dares to break, and the result can only be an exponential run up to some terminal point which arrives when the central bank can no longer inflate."

In both Germany and in the U.S., planned inflation got sluggish economies moving, and helped mask unemployment. Unfortunately, the piper stood in the wings for payment, and payment was made not with earned income, but with paper.

In the first stage of classical inflation, prices advance somewhat slower than the creation of money. In the last stages of classical inflation, prices advance faster than money creation. The point of no return must be cited as critical—difficult to pinpoint, yet mandatory for understanding. To put this in another way, early money is easy money. Late money is tight money. Data presented by Bresciani-Tourroni are not without pertinence.

There was the war—1913 to October 1918. The mark depreciated slowly. People hoarded money and velocity tumbled. The Armistice came in November, and from that point until

July 1919 several factors changed rapidly. Internal prices increased 43%. Note circulation and government short-term debt jumped 57 and 58% respectively. Dollar exchange rates rose 129%. The get-things-moving stage was thus reached.

The next period must be styled August 1919-February 1920, and one that relates to May 1921-July 1922. Here price inflation and dollar exchange outran monetary increases as measured by money supply and government debt increases. Oddly, for the period 1913-October 1918 and for February 1920-May 1921, the exact opposite was true.

That is why stock equities did so well during these periods. Those who have profited or taken a bath in the American stock markets will see the similarity. In short, there was a time to be in equities, and a time to be out.

Bresciani-Tourroni concluded that after July 1922 German inflation reached its super-inflation stage. This stage ran so wild it had to be broken into two other stages.

During one, both dollar exchange and price hikes ran well ahead of monetary expansion. During another, the printing presses ran full speed. Monetary expansion did keep pace with dollar rates and price inflation. The end came, mercifully, in November. Germany's super-inflation blew its lid.

What were the lessons?

In Germany as in America, stock prices held up during the first stage. There were ups and downs, of course. The second stage saw the breakdown of stock prices as the full impact of Versailles hit Germany. The third stage, February 1920 to late in 1921, stock prices recovered. Money and government debt outpaced prices and dollar exchange rates. This caused money to flow into stocks, pushing equities up twice as fast as general prices. The beautiful people made out during this stage. Unemployment just about vanished. The few who took issue with inflation of money were generally dismissed as economic paranoids and cranks.

The fourth stage, from the highs of 1921, marked price collapse over the next twelve month period. It became a near wipeout before it was over. And the beautiful people who were so smart in the third period lost I.Q. points and marks as the hours ticked away. Velocity of money staggered the system as people, one at a time, and in groups, decided to get out of paper at any cost.

During the last stage, stock prices again recovered. Some part of this was due to the fact that law prevented Germans from buying foreign exchange, just as American laws now presume to regulate currency owned by citizens. Stock prices rose ten to fifteen times during the last year before explosion. Unemployment also rose—sevenfold, August to December 1923. Those with old money found themselves wiped out.

At least a dozen lessons emerge from that great classical inflation. Not the least of these lessons is that *inflation forces illiquidity*. People both flee from paper, and they borrow at ruinous rates. They become overextended. When government answers with price controls, the exercise is ineffective. Nothing moves on a straight-line basis, except at the most fundamental levels. There is a tendency of foreign exchange rates to outrun domestic prices, and this creates undervaluations now and then.

The fact that convertibility is stopped causes citizens to lose control of their government, and this sustains inflation. Government *in complete control is government out of control*—hence the complete inability of economists to understand what is happening here or in Japan. Inflation sparks and sustains a merger movement—much as the U.S. has—a conglomerate movement, with captains of industry setting their sails while totally ignorant of their destination. Finally, renters and professionals suffer when inflation sets fire to a system.

MacArthur had no intention of letting events, like a giant ocean wave, guide his action. A similar game plan for Japan would undo his visionary program for designing an economy, a social structure, and fail to preserve for his conquered enemy the benefits of democracy.

Obviously, new debt money can be created in excess of commercial requirements in the U.S. This money fuels inflation, and is likely to run out of control. It has a new twist, however—a deflationary interlude as a stimulant for throwing caution to the wind.

Parasite people seem almost always to be without a responsible bone, and this irresponsibility is being used to buy time—a year if possible, a month if need be, an hour, perhaps a minute. There is no economic plan except to buy time. This has become our reality and our legacy.

How much time, then, can the parasite people buy?

Prophet or Messiah, it mattered little which view the powers that be held of MacArthur. In his mind, he was both—and neither. But he considered himself an astute observer of history. The broad strokes of the historical picture were as clear to him as the tone of a glass bell.

MacArthur must have viewed both this history and its projected results with foreboding as he and his associates went back to the scratchpad principles that underscored his occupation objectives.

—3—

A FRENCH CONNECTION

IT WAS THE CHARACTER OF MONEY that sent researchers scampering to the history books. Everything from barter exchange to cowry shells endured examination until the think tanks finally came to the monetization of thin air—with the concept of land monetization inserted somewhere in between.

During the American Civil War, the United States adopted a paper money standard—the Greenbacks of the Lincoln era. The inflation created by this departure from the Constitution during the Lincoln dictatorship survived both Lincoln and the war. And some consequences remained until the Resumption Act in fact was implemented on January 1, 1879, the date gold payments were resumed.

The great debates that attended passage of the Resumption Act and implementation thereof drew on scholarship rarely encountered today. The logic and rhetoric of that hour survives nevertheless. A most notable example is a short essay born when Andrew Dickson White, the founder of Cornell University, undertook the task of telling members of the Senate and

House something about the role of fiat money in working its historical mischief. White in fact gave his lectures in 1876—and he sketched a picture few with mental acuity could fail to identify. His outline was also the outline of the French Revolution.

By 1789, France had come to the terminal point that always attends structural imbalance in an economy. The tableau economique of the Physiocrats had been rejected. Monetization of new wealth was eschewed in favor of synthetic wealth, gambling, trade manipulations and unwise public management. The short road to prosperity beckoned. A translation into the modern idiom would be, *there was a public clamor to print more money.*

What followed is so classic that attention to details enabled MacArthur's team to impose the French experience atop the likely scenario for the U.S. some decades hence, one pattern almost exactly like the other—economically, politically, morally!

Still mindful of the John Law inflation experience, the French National Assembly—prodded by the storming of the Bastille on July 14, 1789—sought a compromise. The scheme called for monetization of church lands. In other words, the church lands and estates—assembled over fifteen centuries—were seized and divided into units to back circulating media. The first issue was fiercely debated and modestly implemented—no more than 400 million livres in 1,000, 300 and 200 livre notes. The scheme was to keep the money too large for general circulation, but of the right size for purchase of church lands. The new paper currency thus had the earmarks of legitimacy, an attribute that wore away logic the way a grinder eats its way through solid steel. Certainly the members of the assembly were far from ignorant. They knew the danger of rampant issue, how hard it was to control. They understood how it consumed the substance of the worker and farmer, how it annihilated the fixed income of the old people. Not one needed to be reminded how newer and bigger issues created a class of speculators—"more injurious, indeed, than professional criminals," lectured White. One and all they knew that inflation stimulated overproduction at first "and leaves every industry flaccid afterward, how it breaks down thrift and develops political and social immorality."

Historian Barbara Tuchman would call the majority of those in the assembly "woodenheaded," not ignorant. Writing of the deliberations, and speaking to U.S. Senators and Congressmen after the U.S. Civil War, Andrew Dickson White told about the warnings of Assemblyman Cazales: "Never, perhaps, did a political prophecy meet with more exact fulfillment in every line than the terrible picture drawn in one of Cazales speeches in the debate."

It all happened so fast—and yet so slow. In April of 1790, the first 400 million livres were issued. The assembly again met in October 1791, a meeting in which extremists such as Robespierre, Danton and Marat rose to new heights. By August 10, 1792, the mobs were in charge. They slaughtered the Swiss Guard and overthrew the monarchy. Massacres followed, and then—in January 1793, The Reign of Terror.

A steady stream of human beings was fed to the guillotine—and then the price-fixing attempts styled the Law of the Maximum, all to defend assignats, the new name for the currency?

What was wrong with issuing assignats, the new land-based currency? Approximately the same thing that is wrong with credit creation for the purpose of synthesizing markets in our modern era. Neither can deal with the real problem, namely structural imbalance brought on by some initial unreality.

In the case of the United States, the tryst with inflation allowed cheap food to feed the expanding population while transferring the landed resources and earnings of agriculture into the hands of the lending agencies.

The French Assembly missed the point. *It was the product of the land, and not the land itself, that provided the basic earned income with each annual crop.* The land and rain are the sources of crops —much as food and liquid intake furnish the substance for blood—it being the role of money and blood to be consumed by the agencies that create them. Food production turned into money becomes the lifeblood of a system operating in equilibrium because it is produced anew with each season, and consumed in the same suitable time frame.

The initial successes wrought by a flush of new currency—or credit—melts logic the way Oakite eats its way through wrought iron. Mirabeau, once the epitome of reason among men, became so woodenheaded he suggested that assignats be created in an amount necessary to wipe out the national debt.

On September 29, 1790, the deed was done. Another 800 million assignats were issued. Inflation soared, and the government answered in the usual woodenheaded way—by confiscating gold and silver. But it must be stated that most Frenchmen loved inflation—at first. They declared inflation equal to prosperity. And one issue followed the last, usually without debate, much like the U.S. Congress voting to raise the national debt limit.

For a time French manufacturers derived a great advantage. In longhand and on lined tablet paper they calculated their profits from producing cheap to be paid in inflationary money, with foreigners buying the product. Then came the day when manufacturing and commerce collapsed, just as they had collapsed in Austria, Russia, America, and in all lands where credit, debt and fiat money achieved noble status.

Capitalists retreated with their capital. The demand for labor diminished. Business dwindled to where enterprise existed living hand-to-mouth. As business died, speculation and betting took its place. Andrew Dickson White told it this way when instructing U.S. Senate and House members:—"The ordinary motives for saving and care diminished, and a loose luxury spread throughout the country. A still worse outgrowth was the increase of speculation and gambling. With the plethora of paper currency in 1791 appeared the first evidences of that cancerous disease which always follows large issues of irredeemable currency—a disease more permanently injurious to a nation than war, pestilence, or famine. For at the great metropolitan centers grew a luxurious, speculative stock-gambling body, which, like a malignant tumor, absorbed into itself the strength of the nation and sent out its cancerous fibers to the remotest hamlets. At these city centers abundant wealth seemed to be piled up. In the country at large there grew a dislike of steady labor and a contempt for moderate gains and simple living," As the schemers and bookkeeping manipulators prospered, the producers of the country languished.

The general corruption of spirit wasn't simply the personal property of the business classes. It achieved superb expressions among political figures. Leaders of the nation—once believed to be models of probity and honor—became cynical and corrupt beyond common comprehension. In legislative circles debauchery and immorality grew like fungus on a muck heap. The bribe became high art among journalists, much as it now taints men of science.

The new issues followed each other after the briefest intervals. On December 17, 1791, an issue of 2,100 million assignats was ordered. The value of the money faltered, then plunged. And now the substance of the people was taken from them with every device government could command. And the historians have been forced to observe that thousands were saved from starvation only because they were drafted into the army and sent to die on foreign killing grounds. Also, large estates were confiscated, much as a recent U.S. Supreme Court decision allowed confiscation for other than government use in Hawaii.

The Maximum Laws that sought to make real the great unreality of the hour were harsh enough to please any bureau enforcer. In Strassburg, the dwelling of anyone found evading the price regulations was ordered destroyed. Farmers soon learned they could not hold production from the market. Society simply took it once it had been produced. "In irons" for six years was a common punishment, just as prison is now invoked for tax evaders in the U.S. Finally, in 1794, the death penalty became the official punishment for refusing government access to the substance of the worker and farmer. Why didn't people convert assignats into real estate the way they were supposed to? John Stuart Mill pointed out that most people needed their money in their own businesses, or to live. The great issues of money—none of them supported by new wealth monetized at a par price—succeeded in only one thing, namely translating "prosperity into adversity and plenty into famine."

Whatever the laws, by 1795 the worthless paper was in the hands of workers and farmers—people of small means—whereas financial people, as much as possible, transferred their net worth into objects with permanent value. Thus the crushing weight of the fiscal tragedy fell on the former, not the latter.

It ended the way bankruptcy always ends—in receivership. Napoleon became dictator to save France. He immediately imposed the disciplines people would not have tolerated earlier. Napoleon decreed that "I will pay cash or pay nothing." From that moment on, through all the campaigns—Marengo, Austerlitz, Jena, Eylau, Friedland, even through the peace of Tilsit in 1807—there was only one suspension of specie payment, and that only for a day or two. After Waterloo, France suffered no financial distress. As with WWII in the U.S., the sound management of the Napoleonic wars paid for the wars.

Not until WWII did statesmen again draw on the fundamental principle of structural balance, and par exchange for the real creation of money—wealth from the soil. That the U.S. should descend from its lofty triumph into deflation and inflation, not because of ignorance but because of woodenheadedness, will likely remain one of the great enigmas of mankind.

With such lessons securely in tow, the American shogun in Japan could indeed take inventory. In Japan's well structured society, there was little need for the harshness exhibited by The Directory in France. From the very bottom to the very top, society had retained its discipline and its work ethic. The land might well be the source of all new wealth—"*La Terre est la source ou la matiere d'ou l'on tire la Richesse,*" wrote Richard Cantillon in *Essai sur la Nature du Commerce en Général*—but it took a well disciplined workforce to capture that wealth and subject it to the multiplier effect of fabrication and manufactures for a higher national income.

But how could a nation without raw materials monetize its land via monetization of raw materials? Surely the speculative markets would one day destroy the base, just as surely as they destroyed the Mississippi Bubble, the Tulip Craze, and the South Seas road to wealth. The answer is no longer a matter for speculation. It can be found in the unpublished manuscripts of Laurence I. Hewes, former administer in Roosevelt's Farm Credit bureaucracy, and in the record that is Japan's history since WWII.

—4—

THE MASTER PLAN

MORE THAN ONE CONCEPT rejected in the United States—because it did not fit the accepted mode—was adopted in Tokyo and plugged into the master plan for the new world power then being manufactured.

Literally thousands of books, including novels, were scrutinized by the MacArthur team. Two favored authors were Charles Dickens and Erskine Caldwell because their novels illustrated failures of the economic and social systems of the present and the past. They gave graphic descriptions of pitfalls to be avoided. Books about the Great Depression of the U.S. were studied because of their ecological and social messages. One was *The American Farmer*, by Lee Fryer, which was translated into Japanese for Diet and political consumption. More important was the inventory of experience and discoveries hand carried to Japan by Laurence I. Hewes. The trigger force for Hewes and associates was the discovery of society breakdown during the American depression, which caused bankruptcies. As a consequence a million rural people left the midwest for a west coast promised land. Southern people didn't move north, rather they moved into the southwest, and on to

California.

The first Presidential Executive Order to deal with this development was issued in April 1935, which created the Resettlement Administration. This agency was created to address the land problem so that when farmers migrated in large numbers from one area to another, their needs for land might be satisfied. The second basic authority under which the Farm Security Administration was created was the Bankhead-Jones Farm Tenant Act, passed in 1937. The Farm Tenant Act also authorized the creation of the Farm Security Administration to handle a variety of all the different loan and financing services.

Early in the first two years it did not include the financing of tenants to buy their farms. That came about two years later. It provided the authority and the opportunity for Congress to appropriate money for land tenure. In the western region Lee Fryer and associates had a Resettlement Division of which he was the policy head. Included in the grab bag was authority to purchase large tracts of land that were available and to subdivide those and to spend public money building homesteads. Finally the agency reappraised the entire finished farm and sold or leased it to the farmer who was going to occupy it. Bankrolling this process was appropriated money, which was loaned out at 3%. Later support was provided by primarily money that was purchased by the government in New York money markets. This was purchased at between 1% and 1 1/2%. In turn it was loaned to farmers for 3% interest on a forty year payment period.

The agency actually favored lease of properties instead of outright purchase. That saved the farmer from having to pay the 1.6% amortization bill. Basically, the agency created a new value and monetized it by providing either loans and/or investments. This brand of land reform had the effect of supplying value to the balance sheet, making it bankable, with the same government agency being the banker. This was the general idea that Hewes carried to Japan when he was summoned by the MacArthur team.

A case report might well illustrate the point. Lee Fryer recalled handling Boundary Farms on the border of Canada and northern Idaho. There were about 14,000 acres of land there and it was subject to flooding. The farmsteads had to be on higher ground. This caused the farmers to relinquish the idea that they had to have individual scattered homesteads. The resettlement people suggested clustered homesteads that could share water supplies and electricity. In the area presided over by Laurence Hewes, one celebrated example included the Casa Grande project in Arizona, which was 100% communal. All the houses were clustered, which was strongly argued because it saved probably $2,000 or $3,000 per farm for utilities and roads. Hewes also created the Mineral King Project in California. It was located in the Central Valley and Mineral King. When the Bankhead-Jones Farm Tenant Purchase Program came into full force, it handled the scattered transactions all over the United States when a farm tenant needed to buy the property he was farming. This was very prevalent in the south but it was also a national procedure. It was used extensively in the west in financing the settlement of irrigation projects.

The big precedent in U.S. farm financing was cemented into place by the Reclamation Act of 1902. The Reclamation Act was lobbied by agrarian interests that believed that if the irrigation project was financed by the public, it would create enough civic value to justify public support. Therefore the reclamation developments of the west were based on policies which entailed the investment of public funds. For example, Grand Coulee and Black Canyon were developed with public money, and then under an agreement between the Irrigation Districts and the government, a period of five years as a rule after settlement was allowed to elapse before it was determined how much the settlers were to be charged for the water. The water was what made the land valuable. The fact that the government would write off a substantial amount of the costs provided a precedent for writing off the costs of settlement of people during the depression era. That is, quite a large part of it!

Larry Hewes administered all of these programs, and handled the worst of the migratory labor problems as well. He and Beany Baldwin designed and built the migratory labor camps that were suggested by the premise that if you can stabilize the migratory worker, you could eventually enable him to get a farm. The Rural Rehabilitation Act was also passed. It was designed to make all the operation loans for machinery and livestock, all within the matrix of the Improved Land Tenure Policy. Involved in all this was a full scale debt adjustment division which had the view that no farmer could afford to pay his loan unless he could adjust his debts to existing creditors.

This was the pre-war picture, and these were the experiences Laurence Hewes took to Japan with him. The MacArthur team simply took possession of tracts of land previously owned by a few feudal families.

Larry Hewes did not invent new wheels in Japan. He simply trucked to the scene some rather stark experiences, and unloaded the concept of government creating bankable values. These ideas moved off their agrarian plain in the fullness of time and established new uplands of finance that serve and haunt Japan to this day. Lee Fryer noted, "In order to have a meaningful monetization, it has to be done in the sense that it can be repetitive."

Equal priority was allocated to the young adults and the children. The nation's production base—built for the future, not the present—had to be created by the young adults and be functioning perfectly before the children left the classrooms for the final time. Everything in the MacArthur plan revolved around this concept. And, there wasn't much time to get it perfected. In the MacArthur view, the goal of an occupying power following a military defeat was to complete its job as quickly as possible and then depart.

That time came when the diplomatic solution to the Korean peninsula erupted into violence. When WWII ground to a halt by the surrender of Japan, the victorious Western powers carved the world into neat parcels based upon expediency and their local philosophies. Before the war, Korea had been a colony of Japan even though its northern half was aligned closely to China. This division was solved by the victorious powers by dividing this ancient country into a pair of independent entities—whether its natives agreed or not! As could have been anticipated, Korea exploded when the North invaded the South with implied backing from China, which itself had undergone internal convulsions and civil strife. Overnight, the United States forces in South Korea found themselves under attack and a new war was born. General MacArthur was recalled from Tokyo and placed in command of the U.S. response. He met it head-on and later was removed by President Harry Truman when he insisted upon chasing the enemy forces—including Chinese—into the heart of China.

His responsibilities in Japan continued unchanged despite his departure and retirement. Almost eight years had passed since the MacArthur team began the manufacture of a new nation from the fiery rubble left by the Hiroshima bomb. The children at the time of surrender had become young adults and Japan's factories were rebuilt with every function based upon the plan of perfection developed by the American conquerors. A young man named W. Edward Deming in 1950 began teaching Japanese managers, engineers and scientists how to manufacture quality in the newly restored factories. He taught them how to use statistics to learn what any system would do, then design improvements to make that system yield better results.

Quality, innovation, efficiency and pride in controlling costs became the watchwords of the crusade Deming took to every factory in Japan. The world, he taught the managers, must be your marketplace because Japan by itself is unable to absorb your production. It is your duty to study and anticipate the marketplace, create and produce the best new products in the world, and create as many lifetime jobs as possible for Japanese citizens. For Deming and the Japanese industrialists, this became almost a holy crusade. Once the world became their customers, they were building endless expansion for future generations of Japanese. The decade between 1950 and 1960 would be their time of perfection and then, after 1960, they would begin reaching outward. Their first overseas factories were targeted for the decade between 1970 and 1980. After that, expansion would be endless and global. Each nation which became a mercantile captive to Japan would help guarantee the permanent security of Japan and its mushrooming population.

A formula for efficient production requiring a minimum number of workers as a cost-cutting tool to give quality Japanese products an edge in the world marketplace was perfected by making factory employment a patriotic duty in which perfection was an ideal, not just a motto. This goal was stressed in workers' classes held almost daily in every large factory.

Basic accounting procedures used anywhere in the world prove that if an item needs ten men involved in its manufacture, it will be more costly than a similar product involving only six men. In the United States, jobs in factories are not patriotic contributions. Instead, they are only jobs and quality is maintained by an army of inspectors located at intervals along the assembly line. Every American product is inspected several times before it winds up on the shipping dock.

In Japan, where pride is a patriotic duty, it is inspected only once, when it emerges from the assembly line and is ready for shipment. Each step along the line is a work of love by the person adding that bolt or nut, or affixing one piece of metal to another. They aren't just working, they are building a greater and more independent Japan. As a result, Japanese items almost always exhibit better quality and are priced cheaper than similar items made in the United States or Europe.

Implanting this into the Japanese minds was probably the greatest contribution made by Deming and his crew. It gave Japan the entire world as a support mechanism.

The rest has become history. Because Japan and its people were in a daze following the Hiroshima horror in which countless people simply vanished beneath a mushroom cloud, the MacArthur team began its work with what was essentially a blank slate where everything earlier had been erased. Japan had never before faced such a total crippling defeat. The people, because they were accustomed to authoritarian rule, were like sponges waiting for a new source of moisture. For a moment, while the MacArthur team was assembled and began its work, history stood still in its tracks. The results of their imagination and effort are today—over four decades later—carving an increasingly large slice of the world's economic pie. The Japanese have taken the teachings of MacArthur, Deming and the rest of the team and refined them into a high art. They have monetized scarcity into apparently endless wealth.

—5—

THE SOURCE OF PROFIT

SOME YEARS AGO, a socialist wrote to offer $10,000 to anyone who would be kind enough to prove the source of profit. His idea, of course, was that profit was simply the revenue taken from labor by paying the worker for less than he produced. It was all so simple, he said, that even a child could understand except for the atmosphere of intimidation under which classroom instruction commonly proceeds.

We offered a substitute source by saying, *but where did the laborer get this profit*. Work by itself cannot bestow profit. A man in a desert could shovel sand until exhausted and produce no profit. No indeed, labor must have useful raw materials and tools and a society before any profit could be produced to accommodate the theft that the socialist envisioned.

Moreover, production in an advanced society is really collective. The farmer does not feed several dozen people. Even to feed himself would require a homemade tool—a clam shell on the end of a stick—with which to stir the soil. Collective production means that the farmer backed by implement makers, suppliers of every stripe, colleges, publications with useful information, slaughtering operations, grain elevators, processors, etc., can produce food for a nation on a ratio of, say, 1 to 80. Production for exchange through trade channels is the epitome of collectivism.

Consumption, on the other hand, is an individual's activity. It is not enough for the collective production of an economy to simply create the goods. The act of production must also distribute to individual consumers the wherewithal to buy the production. So far, economists have not perfected a bookkeeping system capable of accomplishing this chore, and/or institutional arrangements have elected to ignore, or remain ignorant of, the key to the great economic dilemma.

By the time of the MacArthur dictatorship, principles of accounting for national income and gross national profit had been stripped of logic and encumbered with a fair measure of wishful thinking. A slip in accounting, a simple arithmetical blunder—based on the proposition that an individual's account is constructed on the same basis as public accounts—sets up capital as wealth rather than debt. This lapse in logic prompts almost every human being alive to seek perpetual income without a further expenditure of energy. Accordingly, think tank personnel have proposed and defined an *energy theory of wealth.* The bottom line of this theory is simply that capital is a dead loss, a communal debt rather than communal wealth. It no longer represents a flow of energy and therefore cannot generate income by itself. This "capital is wealth" slip in thinking was cemented into place hard on the heels of the industrial revolution. A clear landmark development was the invention of the steam engine. For the first time, inanimate energy became substituted for human and animal labor on a large scale.

To be sure, man had used nature's winds to sail the high seas, and drawn on tumbling water power in some ingenious and rudimentary ways. These assists, nevertheless, relied on a day-to-day tap on the revenue of sunshine. With the coming of the steam engines, it became possible to tap a gigantic store of sunshine that reached the earth millions of years ago. It has been this fossil fuel tap on which our modern industrial economics have been built. All the early economists came to consider the plant and equipment drain on this fuel as capital. No one paused to reason that you cannot burn coal and still have it. Nor did anyone reason that once coal or oil is burned, there is no way thermodynamically of extracting perpetual interest from it. Yet capital equipment—the energy for which has been totally consumed—presumes to merit perpetual interest. The era through which we are passing has been made possible because man has inherited solar energy stored in a carboniferous era, making it possible to live life beyond the annual revenue of energy.

It has been against this background that economists have conducted their never ending search for a planetary system of the markets. At the time of Andrew Jackson, John Stuart Mill wrote his scholarly *Principles of Political Economy,* a two volume treatise that surveyed the entire field of economics—rents, wages, prices, taxes. Say's Law of Markets still reigned supreme, as it would for a hundred years. And institutional interplay still upset the Law of Markets so regularly that to be an economist in the minds of the common folk was to be a big joke. Yet Mill did more than codify the academic thought of the hour. He brought on a principle all his own—one that has been regularly forgotten and regularly misplaced ever since. In effect, Mill argued that distribution in an institutional world had nothing to do with economics.

"The things are there," wrote Mill. "Mankind, individually or collectively, can do with them as they please. They can place them at the disposal of whomever they please, and on whatever terms. . . . Even what a person has produced by his individual toil, unaided by anyone, he cannot keep, unless by the permission of society. Not only can society take it from him, but individuals could and would take it from him, if society . . . did not . . . employ and pay people for the purpose of preventing him from being disturbed of his possessions. The contribution of wealth, therefore, depends on the laws and customs of society. The rules by which it is determined are what the opinions and feeling of the ruling portion of the community make them, and are very different in different ages and countries, and might be still more different, if mankind so choose. . . ."

Mill's message was transparently obvious. It mattered not whether the natural action of economics was to depress wages, equalize profits, or skyrocket rents. If society did not like the natural results of its economic activity, it had only to change them. Society could tax and subsidize. It could expropriate and redistribute. It could give everything to a king, or it could run a gigantic charity ward. It could give due heed to incentives, or it could—at its own risk—ignore them. But whatever it did, there was no correct distribution—at least none that economics had any claim to fathom. There was no appeal to laws to justify how society shared its fruits.

There were only men sharing their wealth as they saw fit. It was a discovery of profound consequences, for it lifted the whole economic debate from the stifling realm of impersonal and inevitable law and brought it back into the arena of ethics and morality.

Yet even ethics and morality cannot insulate a society from the laws of matter and energy, even though socialists and economists seem to imply as much. It is to the laws of matter and energy that we must turn to learn the conditions under which a monetary system can distribute goods and services without sustained inflation, massive unemployment, makework projects such as war, and the everlasting thralldom of poverty.

The first of the economists in France understood the nature of wealth in terms of an energy flow. "All new wealth comes from the soil," was a French summation. They might well have added, *All profits for society come from the sun.* The key to entry of those profits is simply the dye chlorophyll—the green coloring matter in vegetation. It alone permits harvest of energy on a day-to-day basis, and it was the instrument for that harvest when coal and oil and gas were formed a thousand million years ago. Therefore it is correct to say that the whole of energy that makes the world a going concern comes from the sun.

Life obeys physical laws. It "works according to, not against the principles of the physical sciences," wrote Federick Soddy shortly after winning a Nobel Prize in physics. "Neither individuals nor communities can escape conforming to the laws of matter and energy, however, they may apply them to their own ends."

It takes about one million calories a year to feed a hard-working human being. Food is the first requirement of human life, and life itself demands a constant flow of energy. Only after it has been supplied can men devote themselves to writing books, painting pictures or creating the baubles of the good life. The economic process has its origin in the laws of energy, not exchange. Fortunately, the life process demands more. It demands stylish clothes, comfortable homes, efficient transportation, tools to extend man's puny efforts, and plant and equipment to harness technology. The life process requires production, and production of food and tools requires a tap into the flow of nature's available energy. Indeed, the manner in which production taps into the flow of available energy holds the key for economic balance, that single achievement that could put to pasture both war and depression, unemployment and want, unearned wealth and extreme poverty.

There are certain characteristics of wealth that are often observed, but seldom understood. There are the various commodities that warehouse energy—food, coal, petroleum, sulfur and so on. When these commodities are consumed, they release energy. It is the function of these commodities to be consumed, to be converted into waste—in a word, destroyed. Consumption (and destruction) is not only necessary for economic balance, but a prime requirement. Commodities that warehouse energy are produced simply by combining work and raw materials. And when these commodities are consumed, they yield life energy, waste energy and waste materials. Production of such commodities x price = income. Obviously, production of commodities that warehouse energy is helped along by tools, inventions, automation. When all a man can do is feed himself and no one else, then he cannot develop the good life with theatres, automobiles and vacation homes. Yet the development of tools and equipment cannot outrun the consumption (destruction) of perishable commodities—that is, those that give up energy and suffer annihilation by being what, say, a lump of coal has to be.

Wealth, also, comes in other forms. The fibers we wear, the tools we use, the machines that spin wood and iron—none of these suffer quick destruction in serving their purpose. Still, no machine or building or suit of clothes is really permanent. It is, in terms of energy, consumed as soon as it has been produced. Its creation requires abstinence from regular consumption—a condition that makes creation of capital debt beyond income a physical impossibility. At best, only a brief time can separate it from being washed out. The energy that has gone into its production has—in the very process of production—already been degraded to its final stage. Still, production of fibers, tools, equipment x price = income also, exactly as in the case of commodities that warehouse energy. Permanent wealth is already consumed in terms of energy the minute it is created, but it must pass from the scene (destruction, planned obsolescence, etc.) before there is room for more such production. At a final point, permanent wealth is the same as perishable wealth. And therein lies the problem. Modern money is a fractional part of the debt. It is owned by individuals and owed by the community. That debt represents capital, the energy for creation of which has already been consumed. It carries interest as though perpetual revenue could be obtained without a further expenditure of energy. Unfortunately, the dizzy virtues of compound interest are seen as reality rather than as a physical impossibility by most people. Capital (tools, machinery, etc.) in fact assist in continued production because of a constant expenditure of energy, such as service electricity and heat—and, not least, human labor.

Obviously, perpetual motion is impossible. The laws of physics have decreed that a "continuous" stream of fresh energy is mandatory for the "continuous" operation of any working system, animate or inanimate. Energy is unidirectional, and no continuous cyclic use of energy is even conceivable. According to this reasoning, the flow of energy should be the primary concern of economics.

"In a world which has adequate supplies of energy, scientific knowledge and inventions for utilizing it, and the manpower able and willing to perform the necessary duties and services, poverty and destitution are purely artificial institutions, due to ignorance of the principles of government, actively, if not deliberately, fostered for class ends by legal conventions confusing wealth with debt. Under any scientific system of government they would disappear like smallpox and malaria, by means of preventive rather than ameliorative or curative measures," summarized Frederick Soddy.

The production of wealth—"unclouded by questions of property, law, ownership and complications invoked by the money system"—relies on only three factors, namely discovery, natural energy and human labor. The state of the arts defines the efficiency with which any energy tap can be maintained. Food energy, energy from whatever source, must be utilized on a continuing basis. So-called services—teachers, government workers, doctors, lawyers—do not increase new wealth. They furnish no addition to the national profit because their gains are supported by the rest of the community and efficiency made possible by the state of the arts.

Production from U.S. agriculture constitutes approximately 70% of the raw materials used in operating the American economy. As a consequence, agriculture is both the energy flywheel and balancewheel of the economy, and serves up the potential for structural balance in the entire economy. But to serve its function, nature's input of energy via chlorophyll must be turned into money revenue—that is, made the basis for a renewable money source. That is not now the case. Instead, debt is monetized as it enters the system. It provides the broad spectrum distribution needed to consume not only farm products, but industrial products as well. The bland assertion that society can do as it wishes is true, albeit only as long as breath-taking stupidity presides over government. All who rule lay claim to the legitimacy of office, and all claim to serve the people. But the people—even with ethical leadership—make it impossible for the following reason. We have stated, *it is probably the aim of most people to figure out how to gain perpetual revenue independent of any further expenditure of energy*. This aim authors all the institutional arrangements that make a scientific money system impossible. That this aim cannot be realized thermodynamically no longer needs elaboration. Yet the fantasy holds, and almost all people the world over cherish the idea of a free lunch—hence an impossible social security system, a bankrupt banking system, a faltering dole system. The cost for this fantasy is astronomical, as each convulsion in history readily attests. In America this fantasy means the destruction of a superb farm system and convulsion from which the great democracy is not likely to emerge.

These are the horns of the dilemma between which MacArthur sought to walk. The raw materials equation had to consider the world a global village, and Japan a sort of Las Vegas economy. But Japan had to manufacture its own credits for participation in this equation. Land had to be monetized much as New Deal workers sought to monetize small farms. Once those acres achieved a value—by edict, if necessary—the assets were bankable because new net worths complied with the rubrics of debt creation. And debt could be liquidated by new and higher land values. Required was some mechanism for prevention of faltering values. John Marshall's dictum that the right to tax was the right to destroy suddenly found its corollary—the right to tax was the right to stabilize, and the discovery of this principle became the finding that stabilized Japan. Land that was monetized and held in escrow was as good a backing for money as gold in Fort Knox.

—6—

MONETIZED LAND

IS THERE A MAXIMUM POINT IN VALUE beyond which monetized land as a basis for currency cannot be pushed? If so, what is it and how is it triggered? More importantly, how does land-backed money fare in the world marketplace?

We are told that Japanese real estate and insurance companies can afford to wait twenty to thirty years to develop holdings, thus assuring the economy an undisturbed value base that stays in place, locked in by low expectations of a 3% return on one end, a 96% capital gains tax on the other end. But this land backed money presumes to move into international trade channels for enclave expansion and raw materials security *ad infinitum*.

Are these precepts reasonable?

This is a disturbing question for which no answer seems to exist. It's especially disturbing in light of Japan's heavy involvement in the speculative markets of the world and especially Wall Street. When a group of Japanese investors buy a New York or Los Angeles skyscraper, or a Kansas grain elevator, and payment is made with Japanese currency, is this a speculative investment or a form of the unending conquest that has been part of Japanese history from that day in 1853 when Commodore Perry sailed American warships into Japanese harbors and ended several centuries of isolation for that secretive nation?

Historical events would indicate that Japan, even at that early date, was already having problems in matching its limited land resources to the needs of its growing population. Because it was scarce and precious, Japanese land had already been monetized by 1853 and Perry's arrival just opened new doors to additional wealth. As rapidly as possible, Japan began learning Western ways and the construction of colonial empires being built during that period.

This was the era when national stature was measured by the scope of the colonial possessions acquired, almost always by invasion of some backward land. Great Britain, France, Spain, Holland and Belgium all had colonies scattered around the world, undeveloped and with their natural wealth siphoned back to the heart of empire. The sophisticated societies of London and Paris were cushioned by the riches of their possessions in Africa and Asia. This was a gilded age never seen before or since in world history. Its opulence came from the soil of backward nations invaded, conquered and then milked dry as the wealth of their lands was shipped back to London or Paris as a form of new income to support extravagant tastes.

This was when the monetization of land became formalized. It was a new mathematical equation to expand the value of the pound or the franc far beyond the maximum capabilities of England, France or any of the other colonial powers. Invasion of undeveloped land, followed by exploitation with the natives as captive labor became a mark of refinement in Europe. To a limited sense, this was true in the United States but with one great difference—the Indians were not docile. They could not be made into coolies or char-wallahs. The U.S. solved this problem by eliminating them!

This process of the creation of wealth from the land did not escape notice by the Japanese after a trading agreement had been negotiated by Commodore Perry. As they have done throughout history, they adopted a good idea, refined it, and then used it to foster their own ambitions. Their first step in this direction came in 1889 when Meiji Matsuhito conceived and issued a modern constitution somewhat similar to those of the great colonial powers.

This was only thirty-six years after their first brush with the outside world, just long enough to permit a thorough study of the mechanics of creating new wealth and using occupied land to drain away the excess population.

Five years later, in 1894, the modernized Japanese army invaded China in the Sino-Japanese War and easily overran the primitive defenses of this huge land. When the brief war ended, Japan had acquired Formosa (Taiwan) and the Pescadores Islands. In less than three generations, Japan had developed from an isolated, feudal culture into a world power to be taken seriously by the colonial masters of that period. By monetizing its new acquisitions in the manner of England and France, Japan became wealthy and made its first moves toward industrialization. Its educational system was modernized to match those of the nations that had become Japan's models for greatness. With these moves underway, Japan turned her national attention to the oceans, viewing herself as an oriental England. Much of the new monetized wealth from Formosa was used to build an impressive, modern navy able to dominate the Pacific.

This led to the Russo-Japanese War of 1904 and destruction of most of Russia's navy. This was the point in history when Japan became a world power able to challenge any nation on earth. It also set a precedent for invasion as a way to secure more land and create additional wealth from its soil. One common thread wove through this rush into empire and was the driving force behind each act of expansionist aggression taken by Japan. The population of the home islands was increasing beyond the capacity of these islands to provide food and other necessities. Coupled with this was the new industrial base that was useless without the raw materials to keep it operating.

Japan had only two choices. Either she could join the European powers (who had invented land monetization as a form of wealth) and create a colonial empire, or she could dwindle away into the status prior to the arrival of Commodore Perry. Only one of these alternatives would solve the problem of overpopulation and this led ultimately to invasion of Manchuria, the testing-ground for military action in WWII. In this progression, Japan made only one mistake and it proved almost fatal: after her first study of European-style colonial empire-building, she became preoccupied by her own destiny and remained unaware that the age of colonial empires was dying. Education of the masses in the colonies had made them participants in government, no longer just subjects. This change was illustrated graphically in India by Mohandas K. Gandhi and his endless demands for independence.

Japan's drive for land, wealth and empire contained this oversight, and it was to prove fatal at Hiroshima in WWII. All of this historical background was known by the MacArthur team assembled to manufacture a new Japan that would avoid past mistakes and become a respected member of the world community of nations. What they failed to grasp was the bedrock motive that had driven Japan throughout the period from 1889 through 1941—the land monetization policies of 19th century Europe that were used to offset overpopulation of the home nation, and that had been adopted by Japan for the same reasons.

When the MacArthur team created a new Japan based upon the system of the United States, they failed to take into account the future pressures within Japan that would lead, inevitably, to adoption of an equation in which land equals wealth, but with the errors of the past removed. This time, conquest would be mercantile—not military. Overpopulation would be used as an asset—not a liability as in the past. Overpopulation in the new reasoning was the equivalent of an endless skills bank to be exported to other lands conquered by mercantile, not military, means. Education, not armies, would be the weapons of the future and make Japan a world power. A global conveyor belt was foreseen, one which carried sophisticated Japanese products to other nations, and monetary wealth back to Japan on its return trip. The comparative value of this wealth would be determined by the manufactured value of the Japanese yen, based upon the European practices that were more than a century old. An examination of today's monetization policies will disclose one inescapable fact. They are duplicates of those in use in Europe at the time of the colonial empires of England, France and the other powers. Nothing is changed but the armies that were involved in conquest and occupation. They are replaced by the sophisticated technology of today.

Prior to WWII, Japan showed the world it had the ability to create a heavy industrial base even though it lacked the iron ore for the foundries, the fuel for the smelters or the machinery for production of the factory outputs. Without the conquest of Korea and Manchuria, such a development would have been impossible. After the Pearl Harbor attack, Japan's military drive into French Indo-China (today's Vietnam) and the Dutch East Indies secured supplies of petroleum for her military vehicles and the armada of aircraft. In the early days of the war, everything was stockpiled.

When the war ended, the factories remained reasonably intact, and most of the domestic motorized transport was able to be used. The colonial possessions, of course, were lost forever and with them went the supplies of raw materials. The rudiments of a new trading system were created by the MacArthur team, but were left for Japan to complete after the Americans departed. This was one of the few mistakes made by the team because it left the course of the future in the hands of the Japanese with their memories of recent greatness.

What emerged was a typically Japanese hybrid containing bits and pieces of the American vision, the fixation upon quality implanted by the American teachers—and a heavy dose of the colonial philosophy borrowed from 19th century Europe and adapted to Japanese needs.

All three of these were meshed into a modern drive for penetration of the entire world, using modern techniques but European ambitions and goals.

The result was a social philosophy in which workers are guaranteed a lifetime job in return for unquestioning loyalty and obedience to the goals of the corporation which, because the Emperor is part-owner, has an almost religious stature. This semi-religious partnership between labor and management assures that every item produced will be of the highest quality possible and that production goals will be met without argument.

Because the world—not just Japan—is its marketing target, the corporate employer is obligated to maintain a high degree of efficiency combined with aggressive merchandising in every nation that does not have strict import restrictions. This is a two-way street. The Japanese factory sells a bus, for example, to Mexico, with a free service-test to demonstrate its efficiency. While demonstrating the bus, members of the team scatter and survey Mexico for its assets that might be valuable in Japan. An order is signed for 100 of these vehicles.

The resulting sale may be accompanied by offers on Mexican assets, including land upon which plantations may be developed. The sale is consummated. The Japanese bus manufacturer is paid. This adds to the Japanese monetary wealth. A deal is made for the purchase of 10,000 acres of undeveloped but potentially productive land. Again, money changes hands but this time in the opposite direction. Everybody is happy!

Japanese factories will be kept busy manufacturing the buses, thus subsidizing the cost of the workers. Mexico has made a great deal in the purchase of these buses and also has unloaded 10,000 acres of idle land at a tidy profit. What Mexico does not know is that every acre of this land has already been monetized in Tokyo because it is now Japanese land and, on the books, has had its value increase by several hundred percent. And, plans are moving ahead for stationing Japanese technicians on the land to exploit it and create continuing profits.

This sequence has happened repeatedly almost everywhere within convenient shipping distance of Japan and it has produced several measurable consequences. First, because of their high quality, Japanese products have become implanted in the economy of the host nation. Second, one Japanese plantation almost always generates others until Japan is in a very strong position in the nation's agricultural sector. And, third, the monetary value of Japanese real estate rises with each parcel of land acquired.

The process goes even farther. When Japan is captive to some specific ingredient in their diets or factory inputs, their acquisition doesn't stop with purchase of this raw material. They begin moving to acquire the land upon which it is grown, and upward in the chain of production for control of the central warehouse, the transportation needed to move the commodity, and eventually into the markets which establish its price. This process is, today, well advanced in the U.S., and especially in the agricultural sector.

These are illustrations of the loophole overlooked by the MacArthur team. Somehow, they missed the connection back to 19th century Europe when empires of opulence were created and perpetuated by monetization of land holdings on almost every continent. Was the Japanese fixation upon this belief deliberately withheld from the MacArthur team? Or was it the team which overlooked its presence deep within the Japanese psyche?

To this day, the answer to these questions remains a mystery and too many informal notes from that occupation period are scattered or lost. The most likely explanation for the oversight is this: the Americans were more interested in the present and the future than in the past during an era that had become only a part of history. Colonial occupancy of primitive lands was alien to the American culture and the history they had been taught was limited to major events and dates—not in the reasons why these actions occurred.

Throughout WWII, the American mystique was glamorized as a way to stimulate patriotism. The American GIs were fighting to save mom, apple pie and the girl they left behind who was waiting tearfully for their return. Europe was a battlefield from which Hitler and Mussolini had to be removed. The glorious past when western Europe dominated the world with wealth from its colonial possessions existed, for the GIs, only in old novels or quaint movies from the early days of sound on the screen.

Without doubt, because so many of them were very young, these were the images taken into Japan by many members of the MacArthur team. They would have been blind and deaf to any hints given by their students, in the form of questions or comments. For the conquerors, the redirection of Japan into an American-style nation would have had precedence over everything else and the high degree of intelligence of the students would have been overlooked—or accepted as a form of obedience.

What the Americans failed to grasp was that it is impossible to erase entirely the things learned in an earlier past. The mathematical formulas of colonial Europe at its peak remained untouched in the minds of the Japanese and were refined to include the new technological and financial knowledge being taught by the Americans. At some point not noted by the MacArthur team, a new vision of land monetization took shape and was implemented as soon as the Americans left, in Japan's drive for mercantile conquest within the "hard money" nations of the world.

By the year 1960, this vision was operating efficiently. That was the year when Japanese automobiles began competing aggressively with American manufacturers—within the United States. They were still somewhat crude and box-shaped but they were the wedge to launch a dealer network. By the end of that decade, the U.S. was awash with Japanese products refined to a high degree of perfection—portable radios, TV sets and countless other items easy to ship and aimed at the consumer market. This accomplished several motives: first, it was visible proof of the success of the MacArthur team because Japan obviously was following the American model of manufacturing and marketing. War was no longer in her vocabulary!

Second, the resulting inflow of U.S. dollars into Japan strengthened the yen and permitted Japan to operate in any market in the world, on a par with older and larger nations. The yen was established as a global currency. And finally, world acceptance of high-quality Japanese products was the first step toward gaining control of the raw materials needed to keep this economic engine running. Factories needed iron, steel and other minerals not found in Japan. The workers needed better homes and a constant supply of foodstuffs. To support the coming expansion, global supply outposts needed to be created.

All of these goals, and more, were accomplished by a mix of the teachings by the MacArthur team and a constant reference to colonial Europe at its peak but with its flaws and breakdown points noted and eliminated. There was one exception, though.

An almost exact parallel to the land monetization policies of today's Japan can be found in the old records of colonial Great Britain at its peak. Because their land-areas are approximately equal, Britain provided a handy model for the Japanese to study and copy in every respect but that involving military action. They substituted global electronic communications, the stock markets of the world, and the economics of accommodation, for the armies of soldiers used by the British Empire.

Were the members of the MacArthur team aware of the future plans taking shape in the minds of their students? Was a global Japan with economic "colonies" located in most continents a part of their overall strategy? If they did not include land monetization as a part of their overall plan, how did they miss noting its presence and especially in history?

There is nothing in the old records uncovered so far to indicate whether these questions had been asked, much less answered. There is only that stark reminder by the late emperor Hirohito that the throne might have to wait one hundred years before it could recapture Japan's brand of manifest destiny.

—7—

LEGAL FICTIONS

HOW HAS THIS PROCESS BEEN CONTRIVED of stripping threadbare most of the populace, which once at least owned small patches of virgin land? This question was first posed by Ferdinand Lundberg in *The Rich and the Super-Rich*.

The key legal planks supporting this objective were put into place before Woodrow Wilson left office, and not a few scholars have detailed the legal fictions used ever since to undo a free people and their Constitution. It has also been observed that mere legal ploys were not enough as long as there remained broad-spectrum ownership of land.

At approximately the time of the Great Depression, the cleverness of lawyers became merged with the mendacity of economists to create a Great American Myth. The myth said that the American farmer was such a superman, he produced too much, and therefore the gods on Olympus punished him with low prices in order to bring supply back into balance with demand. In fact, agriculture had its own four horsemen: low prices, poverty, foreclosure, and economic convulsion.

As soon as it became possible, the newspapers of the 1930s started yammering about how the Smoot-Hawley Tariff Bill had destroyed foreign trade, causing the stock market crash in October 1929, and the panic that followed. As a matter of fact the Smoot-Hawley Tariff Bill was not enacted into law until June 1930, fully eight months after the New York stock market crash.

Today the nation is told that farm prices must sink to "market clearing levels" because there are surpluses. The drumbeat is not unlike the one that started with the Wilson administration, when suddenly the nation started hearing talk about overproduction.

Then, during the eleven years between 1933 and 1943, the myth picked up steam. There was more talk, talk, talk about overproduction of agricultural products than had been heard in the previous one hundred fifty years of the nation's history. This was followed by an AAA to prevent production, by farm subsidies to keep the deliberate debauchery of a free agriculture from exploding, by stupidly crafted programs, and by economic duplicity not fully understood by most people to this day. The result was *The American Farmer* that Japanese ruralists read about in the late 1940s.

In order to see the story in full, it becomes necessary to deal with the entire volume of agricultural imports. During the eleven years of 1933 to 1943 inclusive, the total of agricultural imports amounted to over $12 billion. If all these imports had consisted of corn and wheat and hogs and cotton, it would have amounted to:

- Corn—4 billion bushels—two crops.
- Wheat—3.5 billion bushels—seven crops.
- Hogs—187 million head—1 3/4 crops.
- Cotton—53 billion bales—four crops.

If the American farmer had been allowed to produce the amount of agricultural products being imported, it would have, conservatively, required fifteen million able bodied men the entire eleven years to have produced these crops and hogs. If these fifteen million able bodied men had ben employed and had produced that additional $12 billion plus of raw products, then the industries of this country would have been shorthanded and there would never have been a day that industry would not have had the best market in the world for all it could produce.

Under economic law, this $12 billion plus would have turned into $84 billion of national income if the goods had been produced in the U.S.

When the product of one industrial worker is exported at American prices, it is necessary to import the products of half a dozen agricultural workers from other countries to get pay for these exports. When we import the products of half a dozen foreign agricultural workers, we put a half dozen American farm workers out of a job. When we put a half dozen American farm workers out of a job, then a half dozen industrial workers must lose the American market for what they produce.

It is this cycle, which destroys America without doing any good to the rest of the world, that became harnessed in the wake of that successful sales job—the farm surplus myth. In the 1930s, as now, we heard a lot of talk about international trade. "If goods do not flow easily across national boundaries," the saying has it, "then armies make the trip." Yet history reveals that nations which have engaged to the greatest extent in international trade are the ones that brought on both World Wars.

The surplus myth has been used to explain the Great Depression and the process by which home-owned patches of virgin land have disappeared, but a mature understanding of history points to other causes and other culprits. So why not pull up a little history and think this through.

When Queen Victoria died at the beginning of the 20th century and weaker hands took the helm of the British Empire, greedy men shook the very foundations of the world. It took approximately one decade from the death of Queen Victoria until WWI broke out in all its fury in 1914. It was then that the international money changer took over. And these international dealings ultimately brought the U.S. into WWI. And those same internationalists brought a policy to the national administration which culminated in the stock market crash of October 1929.

The surplus ploy was used to hold farm prices down before WWII. Later, the same ploy was used to kill the parity program under which the American economy fought the war. The ink was hardly dry on the WWII Stabilization Act and its Steagall Amendment before the *surplus* yammering started anew. Farmers were enjoying parity prices, this fiction had it, because the U.S. was feeding the Allies. Food and fiber were needed on a global scale so that the brave Russians, British, French, whoever, could fight.

It was the war is a refrain heard to this day. According to this theory, the war drove up farm prices and wiped out surpluses in 1941-1944, but somehow the war was not able to accomplish this chore during the Korean conflict or during the Vietnam affair.

And what are the facts?

The U.S. imported more raw farm production than she exported during each of the WWII years. Nor did imports falter between the end of WWII and 1950. As a matter of fact, parity for farm production, times the multiplier, accounted for so much buying power it wiped out all the raw inventories, made it possible for consumers to upgrade their "hidden hunger" diets, and supported both the war effort and the conversion to peace with very little inflation. The structural balance achieved because of parity enabled the nation to fight a major war, and had the income tax been at a 15% level—much lower than it is now—there would have been no war debt at the end of the conflict.

And what did full parity cost? Not one cent, not one brass farthing, according to Congressman Harold G. Cooley of the House Committee on Agriculture. "The old farm program worked," he wrote in *Food Costs—Farm Prices,* "when the great majority of farmers wanted it to work and were willing to cooperate." For eleven consecutive years prior to 1953, the average prices paid farmers were at or above 100% of parity with the rest of the economy. This was an era of great prosperity in agriculture. The government supported the prices of major storable crops for twenty years (1933-1952 inclusive) at an actual profit of $13 million to the government. This profit was earned by selling commodities—wheat, corn, cotton, tobacco, rice and peanuts—taken over in price supporting operations. Of course, it was known that full parity supported the national income. The general principle had been used by Herbert Hoover, who as economic tsar during WWI saw wheat and other storable commodities raised to and above a parity level "for the duration." During the ten year period, 1930 to 1939, farm prices averaged about 82% of parity, and as a consequence the nation could not rise above approximately 81% employment.

Parity was struck down with the Farm Act of 1948. Suffice it to say that the 1948 act gave rise to abortions such as the Brannan Plan. There was also a renewed hue and cry that the nation was swimming in farm surpluses.

Not all lawmakers took leave of their senses when the experts screamed *surplus!* In 1949 Senator Richard Russell of Georgia and Senator Milton Young of North Dakota—a Democrat and a Republican—joined hands across the party aisle to restore the parity measure for a year. This in fact became the *modus operandi* for a time. Each year until 1954, Congress kept the full Aiken formula in the 1948 act from becoming effective. During all these arguments, England showed more than passing interest in the annihilation of American farm parity. When the U.S. Congress returned to 90% price supports in 1949, English financiers abandoned hope of maintaining the pound sterling at $4.05. Ever since the Roosevelt administration jumped the price of gold to $35 an ounce, the pound sterling had been kept in line with the old gold price of $20.67. Through the rest of the 1930s and all through WWII, England kept the pound sterling at $4.05, chiefly at the expense of the U.S. taxpayer via lend lease.

The British pound was devalued to $2.80—or 30%—in 1949. All the sterling bloc nations followed suit. This action reduced prices in sterling bloc nations by 30% to the rest of the world. As a result of this devaluation, the U.S. became a new high market. In the five years following the devaluation of the British pound, the U.S. imported $6 billion more in farm commodities than were exported. And the surplus syndrome got back on the board. U.S. farm raw materials were perceived to be surplus at the time Dwight D. Eisenhower inched his way into the presidency. "Why has administration after administration so relentlessly, persistently, and unalterably pursued a policy of starvation farm prices, always using the fiction that there were surpluses?"

Georgia Commissioner of Agriculture, Tom Linder, once answered the question. He recalled the days of the AAA. "It was the practice of the Secretary of Agriculture to threaten to dump government stocks of farm products on the market every time the market started up. Citing trade agreements, the Secretary of Agriculture and the Secretary of State could threaten the domestic market not only with government stocks, but they could also dump farm crops from all over the world onto our domestic markets. It was always the policy of the Secretary of Agriculture to greatly exaggerate the stocks of farm products on hand. The surpluses we heard so much about were fictitious or imported or both."

One can look over the hundreds and hundreds of items specified in the trade treaties made during the 1930s and 1940s, and the items given free access to the American market carry a subliminal tag, one designed to give substance to the fiction called *surplus.*

Typical of products given entry under special trade agreements were cotton, cottonseed oil, flaxseed oil, linseed oil, olive oil, palm kernel oil, palm oil, peanut oil, soybean oil, sunflower oil, tung oil, vegetables of many kinds, buttermilk, skimmed milk, whole milk, cream, dried buttermilk, malted milk, oleomargarine and other butter substitutes, cheese, baby chicks, geese, guineas, pigeons, turkeys, barley, buckwheat, wheat, cornmeal, grits, flour, oats, rice, rye, bran shorts, skimmings, soybean meal, tankage, apples, apricots, berries, cherries, citrus fruits, pineapples, plums, jellies, jams, marmalades, cowpeas, cabbage, fruits, etc. Horse and mule meat for human consumption from Mexico were also included.

Thus it can be seen that faltering parity, not a high price, accounts for an inventory buildup—a surplus, if you will. It takes full production times a full price to generate the earned income needed to consume the production. The so-called market clearing "low price" is a businessman's equation, and if allowed to operate beyond a business level, it finally brings on scarcity of domestic production supplemented by imports.

Of the twenty-six grain crops produced between 1908 and the depth of the Great Depression in 1934, the thirteen largest sold for more per bushel than the thirteen smallest.

Japan was not receptive to this American mythology. Quite the contrary, the young men who would become the industrialists in the 1980s, recaptured the values of the earlier American experience, and ignored the new mythology presidents and cabinet members blubbered about as the solution to the world's woes, free international trade and high interest. Not for nothing did Shintaro Ishihara of Sony quote the American economist, Peter Drucker: "Americans cannot live in a symbol economy where businessmen play only with numbers; Americans should come back to real economy where money moves in accordance with real production activities."

Writing in *The Japan That Can Say "No"—The New U.S. Japan Relations Card,* Akio Marita and Shintaro Ishihara, the co-authors said, "Gradually but surely, American business is shifting toward a symbol economy. In addition, it seems fashionable to call the service industry the *futuristic third wave* and information and intelligence is the business of the future. But these produce nothing. Business, in my mind, is nothing but *value added,* we must add value and wisdom to things and this is what America seems to have forgotten. And this is the most deplorable aspect of America today. Japan will do fine as long as it continues to develop and produce things of tangible value; a shift from high technology industry to quick profits from the money game will only serve to accelerate the degeneration of the country. We must take precautions against such developments, providing for, for example, tax advantages for long term investments." This was holdover language from the days of MacArthur. It brought back visions of reality.

In outline form, it described how the money creating function has changed from being based on real production to either transfer of equities or sheer flim-flam. Voices that spoke with reason were ignored.

Writing in the early decade of this century, Benjamin Graham argued for the establishment of a new money, a commodity dollar, that could circulate the same as if it were a silver dollar, Federal Reserve Note, United States Note or National Bank Note. Let Gresham's law decide which money was best, Graham suggested. Under the plan, some twenty basic commodities —everything from steel ingots to wheat—were to be supported by the government. "The only expense connected with instituting and maintaining the Monetary Storage System is the cost of storing the various commodities in the unit," wrote Graham. "The actual acquisition of the commodities does not involve any expense or entail any annual interest charges, for they pay for themselves by qualifying as the backing for currency—in the same way as our gold and silver reserves have always done."

At parity, full monetization of raw materials thus became an interest-free way of creating money on a cyclical basis, with only the physical storage cost as a deficit. Storing gold and silver had never posed much of a problem. Storing wheat and zinc was only slightly more difficult. In any case, this made money meaningful to people.

Historically, the problem is that all the credit schemes and debt formulas and transfer ideas fail the earned income multiplier. To keep the worst effects of economic debauchery from showing, poverty became institutionalized with programs, the brigands and grifters were allowed to gain the upper hand—first an inch, then a mile at a time. No one can point to an hour and moment when U.S. Congress became inherently dishonest, but it happened. The Grace Commission report puts on the table the blunt truth.

The sorry spectacle called the Presidential race over and over tells the U.S. that the system is no longer capable of elevating anyone of real quality to the post of Chief Executive. No one with ability will spend eight to twelve to sixteen years of a lifetime to gain that office, thus it is left perpetually open to mediocrity. All this because old money and young professors and the public at large forgot its ethics, its heritage, and the logic of the Founding Fathers. History tells us that it becomes the legacy of a democracy to dissolve into dictatorship. This is already happening. The form of that dictatorship in our case is *judicial tyranny*. Japan did not forget, and conducted herself accordingly.

Will human foresight and the need for sound economics take command? Theodore H. White, writing in *Caesar at the Rubicon*, may have given us the answer: *If men cannot agree on how to rule themselves, then someone else will conclude that he will do it for them*, the writer in effect said. We no longer need to wonder who is waiting beyond our Rubicon.

—8—

MERCANTILE PATHWAYS

IF THE AMERICAN TEACHERS ignored or missed the parallel in history between these two island nations—Japan and England at its peak—or simply concentrated upon Americanizing their former foe because that was their only order from MacArthur, they missed entirely the most vital part of the educational process. Instead of subduing the Japanese drive for conquest, they only redirected it down mercantile pathways where armies of soldiers are not needed. As soon as Japan was well on its way toward self-sufficiency, the MacArthur team was disbanded and sent back the United States where they rejoined civilian life and scattered. Today, they're either elderly or dead and their personal part in manufacturing a nation is buried deeply within memory. Most have long ago lost contact with each other. Ed Deming, who implanted quality and efficiency within the Japanese industrial machine, is now ninety years old but still active, this time teaching the same processes to American corporations.

The official reports of the MacArthur team survive in the

files but, like all official papers, include little more than the required data and performance observations required by the Washington officialdom. Although it's doubtful, the old files of the State Department might contain mention of land monetization and its deliberate parallel to the British Empire. Observations might be found in old files of some universities, although it is doubtful. At the time when Japan was being manufactured, that task was the only priority that existed.

There are only two places where these observations may be found. One is in old informal notes and observations made by members of the team and that were considered of little consequence at the time. The other is in Tokyo and old British files from the days of empire. A third location might be the old personal files of MacArthur, but they would be buried, overshadowed by his experience in Korea.

The reconstruction here came from old random papers buried in the files for almost forty years, comments made publicly by Deming, and a study of colonial Great Britain, which did nothing but verify the contents of the other data. Unintentionally, the MacArthur team proved that monetization of land is the only sure way to a nation's greatness, but that it may also contain the seeds of its own destruction. If Japan is any example (not including Great Britain) the only way to perpetuation of national wealth is its land, combined with sophisticated use of these natural resources as a tool for unlimited expansion and prosperity. Endless expansion is possible without military force simply by acquiring land elsewhere in the world, adding its acreage to the "home" soil, and then exploiting it to maintain high living standards at home. This process can continue as long as needed—even centuries, in theory.

As the land elsewhere is monetized, it expands the home currency base and thus creates the funds needed for further expansion on an unlimited basis. England maintained prosperity for almost three hundred years by this simple formula and Japan's growth has been phenomenal in her brief experience with this process. Unless she is invaded, it can continue forever—in theory.

How did this formula get lost in history? The MacArthur team should have had an inkling of Japan's plans for the future, but apparently did not. Because the process is transparent, easily visible to anyone who cares to examine it, how has it remained ignored for almost four decades? How many U.S. crises could have been avoided if this process had not been ignored?

Answers to these and countless other similar questions will never be known, but one thing emerges like a spotlight: in manufacturing a new Japan, the MacArthur team did a much more thorough job than they intended. They created a new power able eventually to dominate the world in financial and commercial circles. Unless the process is duplicated elsewhere, in as many locations as possible, this could be the end result.

The aim of science is to foresee, or at least to measure. Grammar school pupils nowadays are taught about things like phase changes, whether water gives up or accepts heat to achieve either the freezing or boiling point, and no one passes on to the next grade without asking and answering questions about appearance and disappearance. The very foundation of logic requires pupils to ask, *Where does it come from and where does it go?* That simple question is appropriate whether dealing with matter, energy or money. It may seem strange to note that in half a hundred texts on money, not one dares ask that question, and the pabulum put out at economic conferences suggests that most money and banking experts dare not answer.

This has prompted not a few students in the underworld of economics—that is, those not blessed and brainwashed by orthodox experts—to conclude that any *private banking and money creation system cannot function without the public's gullibility.*

We can add only a word or two to this harsh assessment—*except in the absence of a system that assures parity prices for the energy-rich raw materials input into the economy.*

Admittedly, this concept needs a bit of explanation. For it is not enough to note that very few people would be inconvenienced if the quantity of money and the price level stayed put. The record clearly indicates that unemployment would literally disappear, inflation would vanish, and the indecency of over half the people living on transfer payments would have no reason for being. At the same time the breath-taking toll taken by official pocket picking and anti-social speculation would be deprived of its foundation and liquidity.

There was a time when some common denominator commodity served as a sort of stand-in for real money, namely the energy flow permitted by the Creator via photosynthesis and man's diligent assist. Sometimes the existing money supply walked hand in hand with the level of activity, and any economy so blessed considered itself stable. At such times, employment achieved a level suitable to a civilized society, and inflation remained in check. Under suitable management, prices could not be ruptured via import invasion. The invention of credit and commercial banking to accommodate changes in the state of the arts, and population growth was not the culprit some socialists envisioned, at least not in America. Removed from the institutional arrangements of Europe, the United States developed a unique commercial banking system, one understood by too few. So pardon us for quoting at length from a brief historical accounting of evolution of the commercial banking system published by the American Institute for Economic Research, Great Barrington, Massachusetts. We think it explains why the American nation could absorb great migrations from Europe, from the Volga region, from Ireland, and from other parts of the world, and why Russia and Europe fell into chaos at exactly the same time.

When this nation's economy boomed after the Civil War until World War I, the markets developed a system to meet the needs for effecting in a non-inflationary way the growth process. The basic principle of sound commercial banking evolved in free markets. The gold exchange values of things produced coming into the markets were briefly monetized, as though they were so much gold, by the commercial lending process, which involved automatically self-liquidating short-term loans. When the loans were made, the banks created corresponding credits to the checking accounts of the shippers, amounts not deducted from other checking accounts. In effect this made the gold standard flexible enough so that the great unforeseen increase in production and even greater need for transactions money was accommodated. These newly created purchasing media were cancelled by repayment of the loans as things were sold in the market. No economist invented the system. No governments created it. Human being operating in free markets coped with a problem for which no solution previously had been provided.

Do not overlook the language quoted above—"The gold exchange values of things produced coming into the markets were briefly monetized, as though they were so much gold"—because this process achieved the equivalent of what we refer to today as parity. Before the Wilson administration, before the enactment of the Federal Reserve Act, parity farm prices were provided for in the marketplace. Import invasion of raw commodities was more difficult to come by. The result was "a system to meet the needs for affecting in a non-inflationary way the growth process."

The problem of an organized society [wrote Carl H. Wilken] is how to bring enough money into circulation each year to enable the people to buy the wealth they can produce in order that all may live on an American standard, provide for the needs of government, and have something for a savings account as a foundation for security and growth.

There are just three ways to bring money into circulation, viz:

1. By the production and sale of the raw materials—products of the ground. That is the dollar we earn.

2. By direct issue by the government as provided in the Constitution. The issue of money leads to inflation.

3. By taxation or some form of credit device. That is the

method we have been following, and it leads to bankruptcy because it dissipates the savings and future earnings of our people.The process of creating wealth starts with the production of raw materials—the products of the ground. Manufacturing, transportation, and other functions of business and capital represent only services which could not be performed at all if the raw materials were not first produced. [As the Sony official put it, they add value.]

The amount of real wealth brought into existence is measured by the number of units of raw materials produced. Society has invented measures of weight, length and volume which never fluctuate and remain constant year after year, but our measure of value resembles a modern jitterbug.

The amount of goods and services such units of new wealth will buy is measured by the price per unit received by the producer of such new wealth. Therefore, the number of units of raw materials produced times the price received equals the new dollar income created during each production cycle or year; the turnover of these dollars in the channels of trade determines the wages of labor and the collective income of the nation.

For example, the sale of 1,000 bushels of wheat at $1 per bushel draws upon our capital structure of $1,000 and starts $1,000 on the way into our trade channels. One thousand bushels of wheat at 50 cents per bushel draw out only $500 and reduce the primary flow of money accordingly. [Under the commercial banking system, creation of a loan to accommodate entry of a new crop into trade channels amounts to monetization of the crop—i.e., turning it into money.]

It is the bushels of wheat, tons of coal pounds of meat, etc., that the people trade. The dollar measures the relationship of the commodities exchanged. When the producer spends the dollar received for his product he passes the purchasing power to the next man and the next.

The units of raw materials—new wealth—are transformed by

industry into other forms of wealth and become permanent assets of society. That is not true of either the dollar of issue or the credit dollar.

These three systems of money creation, examined in depth, readily illustrate the absurdity of issue authority being bestowed on the commercial banking system without some governing device. Once upon a time—and until the Lyndon Johnson administration—a store of gold, the common denominator commodity, presumed to stand guard and say, *So far you may go, and no further!* This requirement would have stopped the debt creation madness in its tracks by springing the trigger mechanism to recession in approximately 1968. When the moment of truth arrived, however, the Johnson administration elected to dismantle the trigger mechanism. The significance of that event escaped instant comprehension by the great minds of academia and government. Admittedly the new public policy could not have been possible without a full measure of "public gullibility." Apparently only young minds groping for answers could pause to ask, "Where does this money come from, and where does it go?" And except for the style common in classroom instruction, young minds would have required an answer.

Such an answer was not forthcoming in 1968. To have provided one would have been to conclude that new wealth—that is monetized debt pretending to represent earned money—could be manufactured out of thin air, a direct refutation of the laws of physics. And such manufacture carried with it the certainly that with the first exchange of this pure "smoke" money for wealth, the money creator gets something for nothing—that is, unless the community has the intelligence to demand something of value be brought into existence and monetized in support of the money creation. The astounding principle that money can be created out of thin air with the hope that its creation will be answered by real production dependent on an energy flow harks back to John Stuart Mill. Mill often ridiculed those who wanted a tie between currency and something physical. Success of the old English system in fact depended on some confusion between debt and wealth, confusion that haunts economic reasoning to this day. H.D. MacLeod, writing in *The Theory of Credit* as early as 1893, pursued the proposition to its logical conclusion. A merchant's credit or ability to run into debt is *wealth*, MacLeod pointed out. Their credit constitutes wealth, and therefore wealth can be created out of nothing.

"How is debt created? By the mere consent of two minds. By the mere fiat of the human will. When two persons have agreed to create a debt, whence does it come? Is it extracted from the materials of the globe? It is a valuable product created out of absolute nothing, and when it is extinguished it is a valuable product decreated into nothing by the mere fiat of the human will.

"Goods, Chattels, Commodities, WEALTH can be created out of absolute nothing and DECREATED again into the absolute nothing from whence they came, to the utter confusion of all the materialistic philosophers from Kapia to the present day and to the first school of economists."

If this reasoning is true, then physics means nothing, and a few superior minds—those capable of determining the need for new credit and those deserving of the lavish reward for creation of wealth out of nothing—are in fact prime movers, not social drones. And the price paid for raw materials matters not at all.

"If we reasoned similarly in physics," commented Frederick Soddy, "we should probably discover that weights possessed the property of levitation."

These several points came to the fore when National Organization for Raw Materials (NORM) spokesmen Vince Rossiter and Charles Walters Jr. testified before the House Subcommittee on Family Farms, Rural Development and Special Studies in 1980. Congressman Richard Nolan was chairman. An abstract in depth of the comments before that Committee illustrates how energy flow, farm income and national income are really the same side of the same coin.

Farm income has a quality that no other types of income have, both men testified. It serves as a basic operating income for the farm, obviously, and it provides the foundation income for rural townspeople who provide services to the farmer—a consequence of division of labor. However, farm income means more. Farm income is our biggest share of the total new wealth created by an economy in any given year or any accounting period. Therefore, it is most of the addition to the existing money supply. It, with other raw material income, is the source of investment for expansion and the foundation for the total savings of any economy. Reason with us for a moment. Fabian societies have been unable to make good their promise that they would make people well. They said they would print money, and everyone would be prosperous. Why are all of the underdeveloped countries still underdeveloped, if it is merely a matter of creating credit and printing money, bonds, bills, notes and other certificates?

In truth, our national earned capital was built from a virgin country. It took generations, each adding annually to the gross value of raw material production, one year on top of the last, to bring on savings. These savings, which reflected a holdback from consumption, built so many homes, so many churches, so many highways, and so many capital improvements. In earlier times people actually waited for the next crop to come in to finish a project, because they did not have the instrumentalities for borrowing from future earnings. However, the full requirement of capital or savings are not generated if raw materials entering the cycle are not monetized on par with wages and capital costs. The missing element in everybody's thinking in the conventional economic set seems to be *cause.* For some reason that escapes NORM thinking, our economists cannot see a causal relationship between raw materials entering the cycle and income at the national level.

We believe that this is so because most economists do what

John R. Commons always said they did. They pick up economic analysis somewhere *in process*. They become so removed from foundation precepts, that they suffer the delusion of the British manufacturer who was told during World War II: "Your factory has just been destroyed by Nazi bombers," and he responded "So what? It is insured."

The only sound way to get newly earned income into the system is not through bookkeeping arrangements, tax offsets, cute little tricks in the financial system, but through the production of new wealth times price per unit. That money does not have to be repaid. The consistent way of developing income is through production of food and fiber at parity. You have a broad distribution here, and it quickly enters into the consumption cycle, so if you monetize raw materials at full parity, it does not matter whether or not the Fed can create credit, because there will be very little need. Two years after the Employment Act of 1946 was passed, the French economist Jacques Reuff said it all: "Inflation does more than complicate the works of parliaments. It makes them a laughing stock and discredits them." It, therefore, causes legislative bodies to sacrifice freedom to soothe the indigestion caused by lack of par exchange between farm and city, between section and nation, and nation and nation.

With or without human intervention, economics is subject to mathematical laws, and this requires men to view the subject from the standpoint of physics and mechanics. "Annual raw material production, in the main food and fuel energy, is the power gear in our economic machine which at all times controls the volume and velocity of industry and trade as finally expressed in total national dollar income," wrote Charles Ray, engineer, analyst, original thinker. "Our annual total national earned income measured in dollars is limited to the total dollars paid for our annual new crop of raw materials of all kinds multiplied by our current annual national trade turn. The increasing pattern of the trade turn is obtained by scrutinizing each previous year's annual total national income. These annual national trade and labor turns are mathematical corollaries of each other, and increase constantly and permanently as the result of technological improvement in farm, mine and factory. "Let us make it clear here that the businessman only legally employs labor and houses and services it with machines [capital investments], but he does not hire [pay] labor, except as an agency. The various groups of labor in order of their importance—farm, mine, factory, trade, and service—through their respective production and mutual consumption of each other's product, hire and pay each other. The initial hiring and paying of all labor starts in the annual cycle with the farmer who as our largest combined capitalist and worker hires himself, hence never lacks employment or fails to produce. This initial farm-labor capital and income automatically multiplies through the rest of the groups in our national economy, at predetermined ratios. Basic agriculture, therefore, literally primes our national economic pump annually and may be said to hire all ensuing or subsequent labor in the whole. *The only exception is that of labor hired and paid by new capital investment in new buildings and equipment, which only a prosperous agriculture can sustain.*

It was this last concept that Keynes and others seized upon during the 1930s, because capital expansion took on *the color of earned income*—the kind turned by raw material production—and satisfied those who created money at a profit. But as Ray stated, debt that pretended to be earnings could not be sustained by anything less than a prosperous raw materials sector.

So ended the Rossiter-Walters testimony.

The question is, *How much of the Japanese prosperity is synthesized and how much is sustainable?*

If it is the function of the scientist to foresee, then it is equally the function of the economist to measure. In laboratory science, such a role would require the discipline to take molecules apart and put them back together, getting a handle on the most minute details and using exactness to determine cause and effect within the purview of the recording instrument, namely man. Any claim that economics is a science must be made in terms of that discipline's capacity for measuring economic phenomena.

A common unit of measurement of most economic activity is money, and this is precisely why economics has its convulsions at regularly spaced intervals in history. A unit of measurement has to have some foundation in physics to be valid. Very little money, and very few people who pretend to understand money, make the connection between the laws of physics and circulating media. The Founding Fathers said, *Congress shall coin the money and regulate the value thereof,* and they put that sentence in the same paragraph with the mandate for regulating the exactness of weights and other measures. At one time it was even understood that money measures, and this was the *raison d'etre* for a commodity base for money.

It is often argued that there is no real reason for a commodity base for money—i.e., gold or silver or wheat or pig iron. The authority of the state is enough, so the argument runs, to bring into being an issue of money to keep pace with the growth of wealth. This same argument holds that national money cannot bear interest, and that all the pretenses at measurement fail because of the dishonest premise.

Others simply beg the question, accept the going concern of monetized debt without analysis, and play the tiddlywinks game of car loadings, auto sales, housing starts, and so on, in an effort to determine whether the latest indicator is a harbinger of inflation or deflation.

Most economists are betting on inflation because they believe in the magic of compound numbers. A small handful—perhaps less than a few hundred writers on the subject—offer a different scenario.

In the library of the present writers, there are at least a hundred volumes on money. One can read for days on end to find even a hint of comprehension. This malaise no doubt governs those who pilot the engines of commerce and those who construct arrays of statistics that pretend to measure every fiber of the economy. From our chair, very few of those volumes are worth the shelf space they take to keep them. For this reason we must—as did MacArthur—turn to other voices in other rooms for answers.

It now seems necessary to turn to philosophy and biology if we want to understand money. People who deify money will not understand the words of the late Dr. Ehrenfried E. Pfeiffer: "Every thought devoted only to money making is deducted from man's cultural development. All this striving for certificates of deposit, hoards of gold coin, titles that pretend to deliver something for nothing—all are a vain part of our lives. The last disease or suffocation makes these instruments of wealth lose their meaning at the individual level." Even an attempt to rule from the grave rarely lasts a generation or two.

Money can only fulfill its role when it is consumed. As we have pointed out, capital is consumed in terms of energy the minute it is delivered. Ponder that statement a moment, then read what Dr. Pfeiffer—the physician, biologist and scientist—had to say:

> *Comparing the economic body with a real living being and its laws with the laws of life, we find only two functions which involve something constantly produced in order to be consumed: the function supported by food and red blood. Food comes from the outside, yet stimulates and supports the body's life just as productive ideas nourish an economic process. Blood, on the other hand, is entirely from within, circulating, being constantly produced and consumed in order to maintain life, supporting the organic functions necessary to growth and reproduction. It is important to realize that the blood is produced by the same organism by which it is consumed; that it is rarely stored and then only in small amounts, for instance, in the spleen; that it is in constant circulation and (this is probably its greatest secret) is properly (not evenly) distributed wherever it is needed. This is the real concept of a biologically sound and healthy unit of organization.*
>
> *Money, curiously, fulfills a similar function—that is, it is or*

should be in constant circulation. It supports and maintains economic life and growth. It is produced by the same body economic by which it is consumed, and should—and here we touch upon the weakness and disease of our present economic system—not to be stored for long or in large quantities (we could speak of an economic hematoma or, in a boom, of its opposite, an economic hemorrhage); and should be properly (not evenly) distributed wherever it is really needed. There should be no anemia of a vital organ, but also no excess.

Finally, the proper distribution of blood is what gives us an understanding of an organism or biological unit and its functions, because there is a higher constructive idea behind it, a higher wisdom of life forces—higher than our intellectual, analytical thought can grasp.

The proper distribution of money—which alone can maintain a healthy economic body—has to be governed by a body of wisdom—that is, the concentrated economic and cultural wisdom of a nation directed by a mutually acceptable idea.

That idea was contained in the public policy of the 1940s, when the raw materials of the earth became the circulating media for the economy, renewed with each season and monetized on par with wages and capital costs.

Ehrenfried Pfeiffer was not alone in comparing the circulation of money in the economy to the circulation of blood. During the Great Depression, William Aberhard, a Bible teaching scholar turned the government of Alberta out on its ear by visiting lessons from the Bible on the constituency, and by comparing money in the economy to blood in the human body. His government lasted for forty years.

His message was the one critics of the 1930s often recited. *The nation had hungry people because there was too much food. Citizens wore shabby clothes because there was too much cotton and wool for clothing. Children starved and died in slums because we had too much building material. Thousands shivered in the winter because there was too much fuel.* Aberhard offered the proposition that this was idiocy, that something was wrong. Moreover, the great minds of the economics profession couldn't come up with an answer. And yet the answer was simple. There was no broad-spectrum distribution of money. Banks no longer wanted the risk that went with making loans. Borrowers never had enough collateral. Capitalists were sitting on their money at 2% interest. Obviously a mechanism was needed to deliver purchasing media to the people. And great minds literally shouted: *Where will all the money come from? Remember John Law, remember The Directory in France, remember the great German inflation!*

And here was Aberhard's answer. The human heart, he said, beats seventy-five times a minute. In one minute it sends a gallon of blood through the body. In one hour it pumps sixty gallons of blood. It does this day in and day out. In a single day the human heart pumps 1,440 gallons of blood. That's enough blood to fill thirty-two oil drums each with forty-five gallons of blood. That's probably equal to the gasoline used in operating a fair sized farm for a month. Yet the human body has only ten pints of the vital fluid. So where does the blood come from?

The analogy to the circulation of money will be at once apparent to the discerning reader. Money must be in constant circulation. It must be produced by the same body economic that consumes it, and all schemes that seek to negate this truth contain the seeds of disaster.

We are told that the great minds in Washington have computed a way for the growth rate to go on forever, all in opposition to the laws of arithmetic. Some of the pundits like a growth rate of 4%. *Myers Finance and Energy* once computed that such a growth rate would mean an increase in the standard of living thirty fold in one hundred years. Sustained for two hundred years, such a growth rate would increase the standard of living some five hundred times, enough, Verne Myers said, to have *the whole population eating Nightingale tongues as their main course.* Yet this is the public policy of the United States, a growth rate based on chain letter doubling and redoubling of the public and private debt. From almost any vantage point, this is the American equivalent of John Law's scheme in the early 1700s, and more clearly the doings in France at the Time of Troubles. In each case the government sought to create money—out of thin air, out of debt, out of land itself—and in each case the state failed because the mechanism did not accept the natural law that says *money must be created by the same agency that consumes it*. Oppressive measures taken to assure compliance with the great unrealities of history—and of the present—are all of the same stripe. For a time during the Hitler regime, it became public policy to in effect monetize the German people. Each birth put marks into the economy, each death removed as much money, thus meeting the cyclical requirement for money creation. The Nazi regime exploded into moral bankruptcy, and the long-term outcome of this experiment went down in flames.

This, too, rated attention as MacArthur's staffers went about the task of creating a new nation. But in the simple depressions measures of Laurence I. Hewes and associates, the occupation forces found fertile soil. The peculiar nature of the Japanese psyche and society did the rest.

—9—

STRUCTURAL BALANCE

IN 1946, THE AMERICAN CONGRESS PASSED the Employment Act of that year, the objective being structural balance for the American economy. Study teams in Asia followed this development with consuming interest, and read narrative and data in Edwin Nourse's first *Economic Report of the President.* The *Economic Report* has since fattened up in pages, but not in wisdom. But during those Truman years—when the last budgets were balanced legitimately and not by statistical manipulation—economic discourse still equated money with opaque production.

Children today are taught from grade one that the earth is a sphere, 8,000 miles in diameter, 25,000 miles in circumference, spinning on its axis at near 1,000 miles an hour once around in twenty-four hours, giving each spot an equal amount of daylight and darkness. They are taught that water covers 74% of this earth, that 26% is dry land, and that out of the 26% only 8% is farmland, 3% of which is suitable for crops. Simple enough, but without instruction to that effect from childhood on, it is not likely that many adults would understand.

Much the same is true of parity. The entire educational

machine has taught the population from day one that supply and demand determine the price, that too much supply causes falling prices, that there are too many farmers when there is any food inventory buildup, that capital consumption for industry is bad, but good for farming—on and on. Unable to handle the abstractions involved, the professors go blithely on their way producing a nation of economic flat earthers.

In no arena is this more evident than the one having to do with money creation. At one time the commodity dollar (for those who can handle the abstraction of calling *money* a *commodity*), was the only form of money. In time the commercial community came to accept certain metals as a common denominator commodity, thus the use of everything from cowry shells to gold coins as money, instead of trading bushels of wheat for furniture or frocks.

In time the fractional reserve came into being. This means the money warehouseman discovered he could loan out more money than he had simply because not all depositors asked for their money at the same time. Sometimes they did, and the run on the bank followed. In some few instances the money warehouseman ended up hanging from the nearest tree. The history of civilization since the industrial revolution can be written largely on a simple chart that illustrates ballooning of the money supply via fiat issue, and collapse of that money supply back to specie, namely the common denominator commodity used as a stand-in for what was really going on in the economy.

Fundamentally, money is nothing more than a fractional part of the raw materials input into an economy. It is not a unit of labor or a unit of high technology or a unit of debt. Labor and high technology can increase the real money supply by increasing farm production, mining efficiency and a bigger timber harvest or fish catch, but this real increase is diminished or extinguished if the costs of labor and high technology are not factored into the exchange value of the raw material input used to operate an economy. Parity for raw materials is nothing more than factoring into raw materials prices the costs loaded onto agriculture by the trucker, the manufacturer, the tax gatherer, and the supplier to the farm. Industrial America and the services industries determine what farm prices must be, and not the other way around.

The national economy is not simply a shoe store raised to the *nth* power. It has dimensions that can only be understood when the abstraction called parity is mastered. No one better illustrated this point than the late Carl Wilken. Here are a few paragraphs Wilken both printed and used orally, as taken from *Prosperity is Within our Grasp* and from a later re-issue called *A Prosperous Post-War Era is Possible.*

"The American People have become a group of specialists and have forgotten that each group is interwoven with every other group in an indivisible economy, with each group a multiple of the complete economy of the United States," Wilken said. "As special groups gain advantage over each other they immediately find that other elements of our economy, those which furnish the markets, do not keep pace with them in the consumption of goods and they all fall back in what is usually called a depression. *In fact a depression is nothing more than an unequal price balance between groups.*" With an ample supply of raw materials and labor, proper pricing of goods and services should automatically create the income to exchange and consume our production.

"It is a simple fact that the financial measure of our economic welfare, whether individual, corporate or governmental, consists of adding up two columns of figures—income and disbursements. Regardless of what our theories may be, these two totals tell the story of our economic well-being."

Here is an edited abstract of Wilken's foundation concept as he expressed it to Congressmen and Commissioners of Agriculture during the months before WWII:

> *Income consists of primary bartering power, which is created by the production and sale of new wealth—things obtained from the earth, farms, mines and seas—and earned income, which is*

derived from wages, interest and profits.

Disbursements include everything on the "outgo" side of the ledger, whether in the accounts of an individual or the government. Even the wages and salaries of those in public service must be regarded as disbursements, since public employees are not producers of wealth.

The amount of primary bartering power, or primary income, depends upon two things—the number of units produced and the price received for them by the producer. In the processing industries and professions the amount of income is governed by hours or days of labor times the rate of pay.

It is therefore fundamentally necessary that the total annual production of goods and services rendered, times prices, plus wages, interest, fees and profits must create an income large enough to pay for all the costs of operating the nation as a business. The total must pay for the costs of government, pay the cost of producing raw materials and for their processing and distribution.

Then as now, we had a nation with plenty of raw materials, ample factories, a developed system of transportation and a willing labor force—all the fundamentals of prosperity—and yet people were jobless, hungry, and farmers were going bankrupt with bumper crops in their bins. Our problem has never been one of production, but of distribution. We have been unable to get the necessary distribution of income, which in turn is ability to buy, into the hands of consumers. Our problem, then, is to put more dollars in the hands of the consuming public. This can be done only by increasing the number of units of production and by maintaining proper prices for the goods produced and of course by maintaining wages, fees, profits, interest rates, all of which supply income and in turn purchasing power. Early in WWI, Herbert Hoover invoked the power of production times price. He raised the price of wheat to an unheard-of scale, and income churned its way through the economy. After the war the bright boys collapsed this fountain of new wealth by driving down prices speculatively—thus the short depression of the 1920s and the long one of the 1930s. But when WWII broke out, the lesson was recaptured. The War Stabilization Act and its Steagall Amendment perfectly matched economic activity to the money supply by in effect monetizing raw production from the nation's farms—which accounted for some 70% of the raw materials used to operate the economy, and involved between 65 and 75% of the harvested acres. This was done via a loan mechanism that maintained parity for fully a decade.

At the end of the 1940s, the Fed and the banking fraternity discerned they could better match money supply to the nation's actual economic activity. The result has been the greatest imbalance and disparity in history, a national economy on the verge of convulsion, a public and private debt in excess of $14 trillion—depending on how it is computed—and work force of over seven million perpetually unemployed.

It is the height of flat earthery to monetize chicken feathers, pure smoke, debt, gold, even land, and hope that the buying power thus created will match what is really happening in the economy. Recall how the French monetized church lands at the Time of Trouble, and that failed because it takes a perfect index of production and money to keep inflation and depression away. Only one mechanism serves this objective, and that is monetization via parity prices of new wealth, preferably new wealth that is consumed, making way for more new wealth in the cycle that follows.

Gold has served as a fair monetary value because historically expansion of its supply has remained very close to population expansion. But its use as a base for the money supply is a poor substitute for maintenance of par exchange.

High technology cannot be substituted without full parity for the raw materials of the earth, nor can a growing service industry. Both are effects, not causes.

Unfortunately, modern economists remove the debate from the abstractions discussed above, and deal in the same flat earth arguments that presume to rely on common sense. Thus the conceptualization among most farm leaders is that surpluses force falling parity, when in fact faltering parity forces a buildup of surpluses. Steady pressure from international trade (based on low labor costs, cheap prices and breath-taking exploitation) has historically forced farm prices lower. In the depth of the depression of the 1930s, with kids dying of pellagra and other hidden hungers, the surplus buildup was so severe that Henry Wallace was forced to burn corn, shoot pigs, and cast fruit into available rivers. Why? Because maximum consumption takes place at full parity, not at low prices. The fact is that agriculture has no right to talk about surplus production as long as there are unemployed millions, more millions on relief, and still more millions without an adequate diet. Failure to maintain parity short-circuits earned purchasing power, hence buildup of surplus inventories, and the human misery mentioned above.

It is not possible to deal with these problems by structuring Marketing Boards for certain minor commodities, and worrying along the matter of inventory buildups, when in fact commodity surpluses are inevitable as long as there is general imbalance, and there are only spot attempts to enforce parity for the raw materials of the earth.

Japanese land reformers came to a basic conclusion early in the occupation. Japan could not compete internationally in the production of rice. Indeed, they could not afford the loss of the multiplier by shipping raw products out of the country. That exercise was reserved for the manufacturing industries.

In order to not muddy the water, Japanese industrialists added their hosannahs to the myth of free international trade as it suited their purpose, and denied it in practice when it came to their farming and raw materials industries. The concept of free international trade seems to have achieved a status of near total acceptance, if you listen to the prints, the professors and certain intellectual bubbleheads. This seems odd enough because there is one principle on which *all* economists agree that argues against it. That principle is the *multiplier*. The principle of the multiplier makes possible the calculation of total national income by furnishing statistics for activity generated as the raw materials churn their way through the economy.

A bushel of grain sold into international trade channels delivers only the raw materials values to the farmer and the economy. It misses out on the multiplier it would invoke were all the economic values to be taken out of that bushel of grain. Population and the state of the arts determine this multiplier. Thus the sale of a bushel of grain into world trade at half parity short changes not only the amount represented by the parity shortfall, but also the national income that would have been generated by keeping the full economic cycle at home. The equation for a bushel of wheat sold at half parity reveals the amount of national income missed by half pricing the product in the first place, and by vacating the full multiplier when handing most of the value to the international raw materials buyer.

It takes no star in arithmetic to start the income shortfall countdown. The national wheat crop at half parity generates only half as much income as that same crop at full parity. This much shortfall cannot churn its way through the economy and obey the multiplier of, say, ten. Half the income from a crop times the millions of bushels of wheat is whistled down the drain by a half-parity policy as an opener. To this travesty must be added the cancelled multiplier—let's say 2.42 million bushels times $2.50 a bushel times a multiplier of 10—$60.5 billion income lost in the transaction.

Thus it appears that a totally accepted and totally incorrect concept is calling for half parity prices and it is exacerbated by the national economic loss. That is a consequence of raw materials exports.

Some 1.275 million bushels of wheat were exported in 1989. The multiplier loss on this crop—based on, say, $2.50 a bushel—computes to $31.875 billion. On the basis of full parity the loss computes to twice as much, over $62 billion national income loss.

This much stated, it now become obvious why increased exports past 6.5% of GNP mean construction of debt. Debt is the usual consequence of selling at a loss. Increased imports past 3.5% of GNP also mean more debt. Combined, these two equations author *steady shipment of jobs and industries to cheap foreign labor markets.*

The professor folks like to roll their eyes like stricken oxen when we present these data. Their reactions suggest that the abstractions are too difficult, that they don't describe the trade situation, that this isn't the way it works. Well, this is the way it works, and we have the public and private debt to prove it. It would be fatuous to suggest that only Japan understands the generation of income discussed above. But we can't possibly be alone in having uncovered these ratios and mechanisms. They are well known and used for self interest purposes, and not to maintain national economy. Bluntly stated, the American people have been made to endure a game of *pretend* for almost eighty years. Because of this, ideas are rated as "true" even if they don't work, just as long as they accommodate the wishes of the international traders and lenders.

In logic, a contradiction is a signal of defeat. The multiplier contradicts everything the traders say—and at last word economists still haven't tried to repeal the law of the multiplier.

—10—

INVESTMENT vs. INVASION

THE ANCIENT GREEKS WERE THE FIRST to discover the correlation between land and wealth. This is apparent from their writings which have survived and the actions they took to preserve their fading empire. Food for their people and for commerce with other nations originated in the land and could not exist without the land. Therefore the land, and not its crops, was perceived to be the source of this wealth.

This simple reasoning for the Greeks was possible because their minds were not cluttered with conflicting beliefs and gold had not yet been converted into a unit of measurement. Gold, to them and other very early civilizations, was a metal used in the manufacture of ornaments. Value was in the ornaments—not the metal. But, using the reasoning of these early Greeks, this metal came from the land and therefore the true unit of measurement was the land and not the ornament or the mineral.

Whether the Greeks made this discovery or whether they borrowed it from some earlier civilization is immaterial. The

Greeks formalized it into a belief and based the wealth of their empire upon it, thus inserting it into the history of civilized mankind.

The Romans distorted this belief by inserting man and his crops within the wealth measurement of its own land and the colonies it acquired. It was distorted further as the Roman legions swept across Europe until they owned more land than they could administer and which had little value because of the poor transportation in those early days, combined with the hostility of the natives of these lands. The Romans made one basic error in their judgment and it cost them the empire they had assembled.

Instead of using the conquered lands as a basis for wealth for the assets they contained, and using them to absorb the excess population of the Roman heartland, they imposed harsh military rule and considered the colonies to be only outposts. As a result, their homeland became densely populated, social divisions appeared, and the empire crumbled. But, even as their empire was falling, the Romans were excellent record-keepers and their work is available today.

Also available is the chronology of other empires in Europe, the Middle East, and Asia, especially in that part of Asia containing today's Cambodia where land-wealth was refined to a high art. These records, complete or in abbreviated form, are available to anyone in the world and a student does not need to be a doctoral candidate to decipher their contents. Somehow, in the Western world, this knowledge has been lost. The tracks left by these very early land-monetized empires were studied painstakingly by the French and Spanish when the age of exploration began. The failure of the Spanish, though, was that they concentrated upon the products of the land (ideally, gold) until a very late date, after the French and then Great Britain had taken the lead. By then, it was too late for the Spanish and their empire began to crumble.

In this country, one of the first to grasp the significance of land as a basis for monetary wealth was Meriwether Lewis who, innocently, discovered and recreated the ancient Greek formula for the creation of wealth. His theories were outlined in great detail in a meeting in 1803 at Cambridge, Maryland. Present at this discussion were Jacob Gomber, member of the Maryland House of Delegates, and his brother-in-law, Zaccheus Beatty.

Gomber and Beatty felt stifled in this Maryland town and were considering a move to the frontier where more opportunities were said to be available. Lewis, a confidant of President Thomas Jefferson, had met Gomber in the House of Delegates during consideration of roadbuilding into or across the Appalachians. At the 1803 meeting, Lewis argued the merits of the use of land as a basis for monetization—and convinced both Gomber and Beatty.

With land values rising in direct proportion to the increase in Maryland's population, Gomber and Beatty sold their houses and headed west, relocating in southern Ohio where they spent the rest of their lives. Fortunately, complete records of this entire sequence have survived and are available today—but there is very little demand for them.

The arguments made by Meriwether Lewis were very simple: no form of wealth can exist without land, whether it is mineral, agricultural or social. Coinage is worthless unless it is supported by the stability of land. The purpose of exploration should be for the purpose of identifying the permanent wealth the land can create, not just conquest for the sake of ownership or to expand the empire. Coinage should be nothing but a tool for making transactions and no transactions can have real meaning unless they are supported by the stability of land. The value of the coinage is determined by population upon the land, and the use to which the land is put to create new mercantile wealth in the form of crops or communities.

Until his death, Lewis almost certainly was unaware that he had stumbled upon the ancient Greek code of value. He bombarded Thomas Jefferson with his theories until finally Jefferson agreed to launch an expedition to map the continent from

Washington to the Pacific coast. Today, this is known in history as the Lewis and Clark expedition and the daily logs kept by Lewis are familiar in any university. What history and the universities have forgotten are the beliefs that caused Lewis to plague the President until Jefferson agreed to underwrite the expedition.

Where did Lewis acquire these beliefs or did he simply piece them together from observations and personal analysis? Answers to these questions are lost today. But, one thing is not lost and that is the direct relationship between coinage, land occupancy and products derived from this land that was the driving force in valuation of the U.S. dollar for well over a century, beginning during the time of Jefferson whose views likely were influenced by Lewis.

In the persuasive arguments of Meriwether Lewis, the land monetization process came full circle, back to the days of the ancient Greeks. However, it was never refined and eventually, in creation of the Federal Reserve System, the U.S. dollar and the land were given separate lives and identities, completely divorced from each other in a direct reversal of the arguments of Meriwether Lewis and the experiences of 2,000 years of history from the time of the early Greeks.

What is disturbing today, or should be disturbing, is the almost exact parallel between the ancient Greeks, the financial anchor supporting the global empires of Great Britain and France, the arguments made in this country by Meriwether Lewis, and the application of these beliefs by the Japanese in today's sophisticated, technical world. The Japanese have made only one deviation—they have applied these beliefs to fit the modern technology of today. They have substituted computers for camels and investment for invasion. They have supplied the missing link that led to collapse of the global empires of England, France and Holland.

The Japanese were stumbling toward answers when, in efforts to expand the wealth and prosperity of their home islands, they invaded Manchuria, China, the Indo-Chinese peninsula and the islands of the Malaysian region of the Pacific. Already, they had identified the relationship between land, its products and population, and wealth for the home island. This is indicated by the public records during the period from about 1932 through WWII. Until it was submerged by news of various battles, Japan made no secret of her intentions or goals.

Through her embassy in Washington, did Japan learn about and borrow the views of Lewis? It is very likely because, at the time of his conversation with Gomber and Beatty, he was secretary to President Thomas Jefferson who had occupied this high office since his election in 1800. Jefferson was a strategist with an inquiring mind and the twenty-nine year old Lewis was one of his first appointments. By 1803, after Jefferson had occupied the Presidency for two years, he and Lewis were in full agreement about the monetary wealth of land as a basis for creating lasting value in this new nation.

A series of actions by Spain and France in 1800, the year when Jefferson was elected, focused his attention upon land as a source of lasting wealth and probably was the trigger that launched the discussions between Lewis and Jefferson. These actions marked the sharp differences between Spain and France in their views toward monetary policy.

Spain viewed land as a place where wealth could be removed; the land itself was seen as having little value unless it contained gold or some other precious mineral. France, on the other hand, followed the old Greek theories in which land—not its contents—was the only true wealth. These differences were highlighted in 1800 when the Spanish fleet blockaded the port of New Orleans, halting all American river traffic. This was followed by a secret agreement between Spain and Napoleon in which the Spaniards ceded the entire mid-continent region of America to France.

In 1803—the same year in which Lewis met with Gomber and Beatty—Jefferson sent James Monroe to France with an offer to buy New Orleans and if possible western Florida for $2 million. Monroe failed to get western Florida but he presented the President with New Orleans, the entire Louisiana Territory held briefly by France—and a bill for $15 million which represented the monetary value France had placed upon this land.

Using the treaty-making powers of the Presidency, Jefferson quickly ratified this purchase even though he knew, as did Lewis, that the U.S. would have to "grow into" retirement of this debt if the $15 million were to be paid without emptying the U.S. treasury or creating ruinous new taxes imposed upon the relatively small population. The only alternative available was creation of new wealth from and by the land acquired from Napoleon.

This could be done only by someone for whom land and wealth were synonymous, someone able to translate his observations in a manner that would make the new lands so enticing to private investment that they would be irresistible. And, Jefferson had to act quickly because the nation was facing that $15 million debt and Napoleon was not noted for patience.

The logical choice was his own secretary, Meriwether Lewis, long an advocate of land monetization despite his young age. Jefferson's appointment of Lewis occurred almost simultaneously with Lewis' discussion with Gomber and Beatty. The result was the Lewis and Clark expedition to the Pacific coast that welded the nation together, stimulated investment in the western lands (including Gomber and Beatty) and established the monetization of land as the basis for national wealth as a national policy that would continue into the twentieth century, until 1913 when the Federal Reserve System was created.

The Federal Reserve System established national banking to bring uniformity into the nation's financial system and it gave the currency an independent life not related to the land, its wealth, or its potential. Because the currency was backed by nothing but more currency within the banking chain and with no relationship to lasting natural wealth it was, in a very real sense, repudiation of a belief extending in an unbroken line all the way back to the ancient Greeks.

By substituting statistical wealth for true, lasting assets it was, in a sense, a sophisticated adaptation of the same theories that had led Spain to ultimate decline. From 1803, the date of the Louisiana Purchase, to 1913 when the basis for this purchase was repudiated, the value of this land had appreciated more than 1,000% and this growth was reflected in the coinage of the nation. During the following fifty years, this value would more than double again but, during this latter period, it had ceased to have any real meaning because the value of the monetary system was based upon itself—and nothing more. The U.S. had become a scrip society in a process that, throughout history, has been incapable of permanence.

History is littered with victims of this policy of substitution. The Japanese were aware of this in the creation of their new society based upon the model presented by MacArthur. To avoid their fatal mistake of the past, they studied everything they could locate and with special emphasis upon economic and monetary matters. There is no question about this fact. Their actions since the MacArthur team was disbanded and departed leave no room for doubts. There is a direct and identifiable correlation between the land and monetary policies they have adopted, and those of Jefferson and Lewis. Suggestions of the Napoleonic codes can also be found in the actions they have taken.

Their actions and policies are uncomfortably similar to those taken by Jefferson, Meriwether Lewis, Napoleon and those who came before them in civilized history, and especially the construction of the British Empire to a level of greatness never rivaled before or since.

Meantime, the United States is in agonies of indecision over monetary dislocations, while the market value of the land is declining steadily. And, an increasing mercantile invasion of the U.S. by Japan is playing havoc with our statistical monetary wealth.

Could MacArthur have foreseen this as a future possibility? Where were our universities when Japan quietly monetized its land, copying faithfully the formula codified by Thomas Jefferson and based upon numerous historical parallels? Is it too late to restore the U.S. to the formula that worked so well here for so long and that is now being illustrated by the Japanese? Is the United States the victim of history, too much tinkering, or just national ignorance combined with good intentions? There are no answers to these questions and, in fact, the questions haven't even been asked in Washington, the universities, or elsewhere.

Unintentionally, the MacArthur team that manufactured a new Japan created an inquisitive monster whose major advantage was that it had its beginning on a blank sheet of paper and with a willing populace. In its manufacture, the mistakes of the past by other powers could be avoided and a model governmental society could be created.

Now that our creation has reached national adulthood, is there anyone left over here who understands economic history and its consequences that are inevitable if certain choices are made? This is the leftover question that remains after the MacArthur papers are studied, after the Jeffersonian decisions are reviewed along with the arguments of Meriwether Lewis, after the experiences of Spain and Napoleonic France are compared, after the construction of the British Empire is examined, and after the policies of ancient Greece are reviewed.

Or, with the United States facing a $4 trillion-plus budget debt in the federal government, declining real estate values in much of the nation, higher taxes a certainty, and a measurable cleavage within society as it separates itself into "haves" and "have-nots," is it too late for such an examination?

The answers to these, and especially the final question, will be known before the year 2000—whether or not all of the other questions are examined and answers are learned.

—11—

MECHANISM FOR EXPANSION

MUCH LIKE THE SORCERER'S APPRENTICE, MacArthur's team showed the Japanese how to make it rain, but they forgot to show their former enemies how to turn it off. The rain in this case was money. And the mechanism for making it rain is credit, land evaluation and the magic of 70% to 120%, the amount banks stand ready to loan on collateral that seems to grow in value like money on a tree. The precise mechanism has been compared to the Texas thrift scam, a mechanism that took a piece of property from ground zero to the stratosphere via sales and bids that served as ratchets for a real estate *upsadasium* game. What started as a simple process of conferring value on land during an agrarian reform—making the asset bankable—has now blossomed into a mechanism for expansion without war, and for achievement of all of Japan's WWII objectives without firing a shot.

Any sale of property confers new values on surrounding property because the myth that there is a fantastic shortage of space is alive and well. Yet there are tens of thousands of acres zoned agricultural in Tokyo. Yukio Noguchi, an economics professor at Hitotsubashi University, computes that the average amount of floor space in Tokyo homes is only 40% of the maximum allowed by law.

Tokyo has 89,000 acres of farmland, 56,000 acres of vacant land, and some 15,000 acres of state-owned land. Thus Japan on inspection appears to be a land of two-family houses, three generation mortgages and four hour commutes, all while Tokyo has a land area the size of Chicago awaiting development.

But development is slow because it costs almost nothing to sit on land, yet that land and a good line of credit is the key to wealth beyond the dreams of avarice. Families with property can borrow up to 120%, pay no interest for two years, sell stocks or acquisitions at a profit and pay off the loan.

International pundits have called this process "monetization of land," and defined it as the miracle blessing of the ages—and so it seems. Certainly taxes on land are small, about 0.1% of the market value. Small residential plots and agricultural land is taxed even less. A 1921 Japanese law stabilizes rents and limits increases to increments of 10% every two years. Tenants cannot be evicted under the law. In Tokyo a building is valued at about one-tenth the value of the land on which it sits, just the opposite of the United States. Capital gains taxes in Tokyo can bite off as much as 96% of real estate transaction profits, and unless loopholes around this bite can be found, sales stand still —unless the real estate cycle has come full turn. These cycles have enjoyed their seven and eight year swings for some thirty years, the last peak arriving in 1987. In that year prices and values jumped 75%, whether the property sold or not. Some plots reportedly sold four and five times during, before, and after the 1987 peak, with Texas thrift scam style accounting for an appreciation of 500%.

Each turn of the ratchet raised borrowing power to new heights, giving the world a suggestion that a perpetual motion machine had been found. In Tokyo they have a term for a new type of operator—the *yakuza,* or gangsters. Using strong arm tactics, these entrepreneurs persuade reluctant sellers to vacate their wooden homes in the path of progress.

This willingness of lenders to create money out of thin air on the basis of real property assets, and the propensity of low interest and high taxes to hold values as backing—much like Fort Knox gold—has created breath-taking absurdities. Mitsubishi Estate's land holdings in Marunouchi have been calculated at a worth of $21.1 billion. Gold isn't worth as much computed on a meter by meter basis six inches deep.

News reports current at the turn of the decade indicated that Japan's theoretical land value surpassed by four times that of all land in the United States, a nation almost twenty-five times larger than Japan. The calculated cash value of the Chiyoda-ku ward in downtown Tokyo could in theory buy all of Canada. Land in the Ginza shopping district was selling for $250,000 a square meter in 1988.

The economy effect of Japanese financial, tax and land use policy has been to guarantee that speculative values would stay in orbit, never to decline by more than a modest fraction in any accounting period. *Harvard Business Review* has compared this sequence to commercial and residential prices in Los Angeles, West Los Angeles and even Orange County rising 200% or 300% or 400% in, say, three years, with banks salivating to loan 80% of the new value for investment or stock market plunges. Whether public policy is strong enough to hold in place the value of pure smoke money can be answered only by history. A mature sense of values suggests that ultimately mathematical ambition and physical possibility will part company.

Thus it seems one myth is holding up the Japanese money machine while a second myth is pulling down the American money machine.

The U.S. enchantment with higher taxes has run exactly counter to the general atmosphere in Japan.

We have already pointed out that a modest 15% income tax

during WWII could have paid for the war, production times price and the multiplier delivering enough income into the economy to provide the base for a tax bite. But with taxes moving up to 54% of gross national income circa 1990—social security and all tax forms included—the investment potential for job creation simply is no longer available in the U.S. Warren Brooks of *Detroit News*, has concluded—correctly we believe—that for every $100 property taxes go up, real values fall by $1000, and vice versa. "This is neither mystical nor theoretical. It operates as accounting law." Indeed, the relationship is no different than the connection between bond prices and interest rates. Rates in effect are a tax on borrowing. Higher rates mean lower bond revenues, and vice versa.

Application of this arithmetic can be seen with each spate of tax increases. Each time the Congress, in its wisdom, increases taxes, say $30 billion, the action effectively destroys the investment needed by the nation for a full year. A complete kill-off of investment for a year is an insurance policy for a stock market drop of from three hundred to five hundred points. Thus the anatomy of the Japanese miracle comes clear. Whether its monetization of land will prove more effective in the long term than the assignat monetization of the French remains to be seen.

Before the dust settles on the next century, MacArthur's gift may be viewed as a "Remember Pearl Harbor" memento, delivered in person.

In the meantime the U.S. remains vulnerable in spite of the fact that only a marginal production capability supports the speculative monetization of commercial land.

The key seems to be that Japanese land is the only tradable value not subject to the discipline of international markets. Accordingly, values are what the Japanese say they are—the theory being that the higher the prices, the more brilliant Japan's future. And in theory the money machine can be cranked up enough to buy up the entire world.

Unfortunately a cloud no bigger than the palm of a hand has already appeared—Donald Trump-like failures in a Japanese real estate market that brooks no failure.

There is a truism often attributed to John Maynard Keynes. It says the inevitable never happens, the unexpected does. This comes terribly close to saying, *all absolutes are false, including this one.*

At one time communism seemed to be the answer for the great minds at Cambridge, Keynes included. Yet by the time Josef Stalin took command of the U.S.S.R., the highest inner circles knew communism to be a failure. Aleksandr Solzhenitsyn related this intelligence in volume two of his *Gulag Archipeligo.* He also explained that Stalin closeted himself for several days with a Turkish businessman named Naftaly A. Frenkel, an old friend.

Frenkel reasoned, as do most businessmen, that values and profits are predatory, always achieved at the expense of others. He told Stalin that in order for communism to fly, it would be necessary to get free labor. This conclusion achieved, the two then proceeded to construct their syllogism in reverse. Frenkel pointed out that not just any labor would do. This free labor had to know how to do things—and thus the judgment was made to draw up a list of engineers. *Now,* said Frenkel, *arrest every seventh one!* These workers would bring their own energy into the system. And the system would harvest this energy, giving all those who confessed to choreographed crimes only thin cabbage soup and minimal support for life. Most would be dead in a year or two.

This free labor built and staffed the Gulag. As the Gulag expanded, coal, minerals, gold—especially gold—and timber met the raw materials requirements of what pundits called "the future now." There was a problem with this business equation. It did not answer the requirements of economics. Because free labor was used, raw materials failed to generate the base income that could—via the multiplier—hoist up the national income. As a consequence the Soviet economy always operated without an adequate social surplus, or a proper profit for the system. Cheap labor in fact sounded the death knell for communism that far back.

It was only a decade or two before the Stalin era that Henry Ford reasoned, *If we do not raise the industrial wage to fifty cents an hour, the worker will never be able to own a Model T car.* Accordingly, Ford took the lead in raising the American industrial wage to fifty cents an hour. Others accepted this reasoning and joined the effort. On this basis the United States built the biggest steel industry, the biggest auto industry, the biggest just-about-everything.

There were depressions called panics, and then there came that engineered depression of the 1930s, which was crafted by business people who wanted the disparity required by free trade. There were also periods of structural balance. These were created by stabilization measures, by raw materials prices in line with wages and capital costs, and by an understanding that free labor was a delusion of maximum dimension because the absence of income short-circuits the exchange equation. Today, half the world is coming unglued because the act of production is not creating and distributing the credits needed for consumption.

It took over seven decades for Stalin's economic error to undo communism. And yet the U.S. is following Frenkel's advice in its own dumb way. According to many Congressmen and an incumbent President, the United States too needs free labor—or at the bare minimum, cheap labor. A rationale for this Stalinesque conclusion has now arrived in the public prints: a free trade agreement with Mexico will lessen "pressure on workers to cross the Rio Grande in search of work in the United States."

Kansas Congressman James Slattery has literally rhapsodized about the free trade agreement. "It would lock in reforms by President Carlos Salina de Gortari's government that have transformed Mexico's economy from one of the world's most protected to one of the more open. It would also provide U.S. companies with a vast labor pool and a more stable investment climate. And, assuming that its standard of living would rise, Mexico eventually could provide a ready market for U.S. goods and services, such as the agricultural exports which dominate the Kansas economy."

We will pause here to permit our readers to digest this brand of conjectural economics. Few will have to be reminded that this oft-repeated scenario has never worked out as now—to some—seems inevitable. In fact the cheap labor, cheap raw materials objective has always ended in convulsion, and will end up in convulsion again.

Even a casual trip to Mexico will bring the dimensions of free trade into focus. At the border town of Reynosa, trucks line up as far as one can see, all headed into Mexico. These trucks are loaded with raw materials, parts, components, so that business firms can absorb the blessings of $33 a week labor—the American counterpart of Stalin's free labor. Businessmen like the arrangement because they think as businessmen must. They like cheap costs in Mexico and the prospect of selling goods in U.S. markets for prices that might be proper if manufacturers operated at the U.S. industrial wage level.

Congressmen do not generally define the scope of free trade exports. They fail to explain that foreign sales mean foreign gifting. Loans, guarantees and gifts—that's the name of the game. "Exports to Mexico are terribly important to the Kansas economy," opines the Congressman. "Mexican demand for both of these commodities is likely to increase as Mexico shifts its labor pool from agriculture to industry"—wishful thinking all of it.

We have here more than a failure to communicate. We have in fact convulsion in the making, and no one in charge who knows how to manage that convulsion.

Civilizations run in theory periods, not cycles. We have lived through a theory period that saw the Soviet Union recite its nonsense for almost eight decades before that brand of convoluted reasoning undercut itself.

Now we see two of the world's economies—Japan and the U.S.—each with a theory period rushing toward convulsion.

The present American economic theory period expects a foreigner to conjure up money with which to buy without producing something that has to be sold. The Japanese model for creating money out of thin air and harvesting revenue from one-way trade is similarly on a collision course with history. And when the worlds collide, the multitudes mentioned in the biblical *Book of Joel* will no doubt have ready their unexpected answers.

—12—

THE DRUMBEAT OF HISTORY

THE ECONOMIST COLIN CLARK ONCE CONCLUDED that no nation could tax more than between 25 and 30% of gross national income without bringing on fantastic adjustments in political and institutional arrangements.

The drumbeat of history has rolled out the fact that no nation can compound public and private debt *ad infinitum*. The wreckage caused by high interest has been documented throughout history, starting with the digs that uncovered the ziggurats or temples of ancient Babylon. Here archaeologists recovered clay tablets that were an integral part of an economic system developed by the priests of Baal. Their system relied on short-changing the producers of real wealth, then loaning them the wherewithal to put in a new crop. By requiring interest the priests of Baal engineered default and bankruptcy. Because there was always less money in existence than the amount needed to retire the loans and pay the interest, the farmers had to forfeit their collateral. First the priests of Baal took livestock, then land, then the children of the family were sold into slavery—next the wife, and finally the farmer himself. Joseph's enslavement of the children of Israel on behalf of the Pharaoh was little different. Through the centuries governments have been taken over by clever lenders so that money could be created out of thin air, with borrowers—in the aggregate—taking on the impossible.

This business of borrowing money into circulation, then withholding more money creation to make payment and debt service impossible, haunted Persia, cursed Greece and Rome, annihilated the defense of Carthage, and presided over death and wars from the days of *Deuteronomy* to the present. Each year between 1916 and 1946, for instance, there had been an increase in the public and private debt—this to make the payment of interest possible. In 1946 the public and private debt stood at $396.6 billion—down from $405.9 billion. The economic advisers saw these figures as the harbinger of depression, and yet there was no depression. In fact the economy had earned enough profit during the previous four years to literally pay for World War II. The mechanism was simple enough. Production times price generated income, and with prices in all sectors regulated at a profitable level, the act of growing corn and wheat and building war materiel brought national earned income back to a prosperous pre-1929 level. Some $200 billion in debt expansion to fight World War II really hadn't been required. This made the management of WWII the only significant economic development between the days of the Baal priests and the present, and Truman's luck was there to nail down the benefits.

This record suggests a fundamental error in the business of using debt to drive the economy, rather than earned income and profits.

The Japanese experience and its American counterpart seem both to suggest the requirement for cyclical creation of money to balance the physical economy.

A recent USDA study documents the fact that American farmers are producing 240% of 1930 production in order to feed one hundred million more people than existed in 1930, and doing it for less "real" adjusted for inflation dollars than the agricultural sector earned for 100% of production in 1930. The farmers characterized as bastardized, money-grubbers who feed wantonly at the public trough of tax dollars annually—at the expense of the consumer—have in reality been feeding the one hundred million increase in population free of charge. However, when one accounts for the diminished farm population, and ignores completely the 140% increase in bushels and pounds of farm production, the farm family today is earning somewhere near what a counterpart farm family earned in 1930. The problem is this never reaches the classroom of our land grant colleges. It is a deep dark secret. Not many people bother to look at or care about its consequences in rural America.

When W. Stanley Jevons rediscovered Cantillon about the time Andrew Jackson was President in the U.S., he concluded that Cantillon's analysis of the circulation of wealth anticipated by seventy years J.B. Say's Law of Markets. He also noted that Cantillon's precept of balance of payments between country and city, between country and country, described the root of inflation and the cause of periodic convulsion. It must be remembered that Cantillon was a contemporary of John Law, who like most modern economists believed that wealth could be created with an act of the will, and out of nothing.

It was Cantillon's assertion that all new wealth came from the soil—and that labor enabled its production—that made a distinction between the material cause and the formal cause (in terms of Aristotelian philosophy). Quesnay's fundamental doctrine *"a terre est l'unique source des richesses"* came straight from Cantillon's *Essai*, just as did Adam Smith's assertion that a nation was required to develop its agriculture first, its manufacturing second, and its trade last, and not to let any of them languish.

The question at this juncture has to be—*Is monetization of speculative land values an answer to coinage, once considered the politics of scarcity?* Japan's experience has its own suggestion. So far superior worker discipline and tacit acceptance of half the international exchange equation seems to support the money creation system MacArthur put into place. Yet, standing in the wings, is the suggestion that this is the British experience and the empire on which the sun will set all over again.

AFTERWORD

IN *RAW MATERIALS ECONOMICS, A NORM PRIMER* (NORM being an acronym for National Organization for Raw Materials), Charles Walters Jr. pointed to the world of make-believe in which we live. This mode of thought, this theory-period thinking, seems to have captured the emotions and intellects of all. That theory period has ignored the laws of physics and structured—in the mind's eye, at least—an exponential growth based on an abstraction that is quite impossible.

Our own theory period leading to convulsion is not the first, as we have seen in the short chapters of this book. Charles Mackay, writing in *Extraordinary Popular Delusions and the Madness of Crowds,* detailed how nation after nation has "become simultaneously impressed with one delusion, and run after it, till their attention is caught by some new folly more captivating than the first. We see one nation suddenly seized, from its highest to its lowest members, with a fierce desire of military glory; another as suddenly becoming crazed upon a religious scruple; and neither of them recovering its senses until it has shed rivers of blood and sowed a harvest of groans and tears, to be reaped by its posterity. . . . Money, again, has often been a cause of the delusion of multitudes. Sober nations have all at once become desperate gamblers, and risked almost their existence upon the turn of a piece of paper. . . . Men, it has been well said, think in herds; it will be seen they go mad in herds, while they only recover their senses slowly, and one at a time."

The two delusions of our time have been set out clearly, we hope, in this short volume, one by implication, one by name.

The first is the "fast track" of GATT, the General Agreements on Tariffs and Trade. This delusion has its own nomenclature—*trading partners, global village, free trade, laissez faire*. Under this theory the United States presumes to sell its $18,000 automobiles and foreign-made TV sets to nations with industrial wages ranging from eight cents an hour upward, with only a rare "trading partner" even approaching the U.S. industrial wage rate of $10.00 an hour. Needless to say, most serious transactions require loan guarantees and outright gifts to these trading partners so that they can buy. If anything, a new term must be installed in the grammar of GATT—namely *gifting*.

Business may profit, but the American economy bleeds profusely. That is why *Raw Materials Economics* was forced to observe that when foreign sales account for more than 6.5% of the U.S. national income, at that point factories start moving out, income and employment falter, and convulsion is in the making. The American economic system set up by the Founding Fathers precluded these unhappy results, but this system was swept away at the time of the Wilson administration, with the delusions of our times to follow.

The second delusion is the Japanese money factory, which has been explained herein. The MacArthur dictatorship, in retrospect, was more a trigger mechanism that a cause. The aim of economics is not only to understand, but to predict. Economics must not only describe the life process involved in producing, distributing and consuming wealth, but must join the observations into working realities called laws. These laws must enable man to predict, then to design. Cause and effect, whether managed or natural, must be understood, or the science of economics is less than nothing. Cause and effect can range all the way from "water runs downhill" to the citation by R. H. Tawney in *Religion and the Rise of Capitalism* that "exploitation of the weak by the powerful, organized for the purpose of economic gain, buttressed by imposing systems of law, and screened by decorous draperies of virtuous sentiment and resounding rhetoric, has been a permanent feature in the life of most communities that the world has yet seen."

Japan understands that *global village* is a euphemism, not a reality. Japan sees the American idea of *free trade* as a delusion of the simple-minded and a banner of the business opportunist. Japan has taken in—and given room and board—to the ideas that made America great, namely quality, efficiency and national pride. The oligarchy that runs Japan has also mastered the incredibly simple, albeit mostly uncomprehended, rules for creating H. D. MacLeod-style wealth out of thin air. This alchemy—more than international trade—contains the seeds of convulsion. Edward Deming has been mentioned. Fleshed out and further explained, the Deming contribution would have required some reference to Carl Shoup, the Columbia University professor, who used classical procedures for management of inflation, at the same time delivering the benefits of one-way international trade. Joseph Dodge, a Detroit banker, understood the requirement for profits and savings, and secured the benefits of their generation via a tax-free savings plan. Withal, it was Deming who taught the Japanese to answer money creation with quality production. He was not able to explain the limits of abstract wealth creation and that this creation had ultimately to bow to physical reality in a very real world.

Quality of population and a special work ethic can no doubt support the dizzy accomplishments of Asia's four tigers—Taiwan, Hong Kong, Singapore and Korea—which have parlayed an American myth into temporary largess. But in the final analysis, weight obeys the laws of gravity, not levity, and monetized air simply evaporates back into the money heaven from which it came.

The roads to economic convulsion are many, and those with the intelligence to manage full-scale disintegration are few.

—APPENDIX—

REFLECTIONS

by Lee Fryer

ABOUT FIFTY YEARS AGO, Jerry Voorhis, a young Congressman from California, produced a seminal book entitled, *Out Of Debt, Out Of Danger.* It was the first valid description of the process used by private enterprise to create money, in this case by the Federal Reserve System which, as Voorhis explained, is a private business institution owned by its member banks and is only peripherally controlled by the United States government.

The members of the Board of Governors of the Federal Reserve System are nominated by the President of the United States and confirmed by the Senate—a civic/political process. Thereafter, they function as directors of our "National" bank.

Upon witnessing the incompetence of this system in protecting the public against the ravages of the Great Depression of the 1930s, Jerry Voorhis explained this debacle. Then, convinced that our country needs a central public bank clearly mandated to protect the public interest, he proposed an Act of Congress nationalizing the Federal Reserve System, providing it with authority and responsibility for carrying out this mission.

In *Out Of Debt, Out Of Danger,* Voorhis described the dynamic process by which over 90% of all money in the United States is "coined" and fed into the national economy. This is done via loans made by banks to companies, organizations and people. It is like this: you, Jim Doe, walk into your local bank and say to the loan officer, "I'd like to borrow $1,000." Whereupon, using the bank's current loan criteria, the bank approves your loan and credits this money to your checking account. That transaction creates *new* money, just as good for spending as if it were ten $100 bills.

A similar process of "monetizing" credit occurs when your local video store, responding to steeply rising demands for video cassettes, gets a loan of $50,000 for expansion. That $50,000 moves into the local and trade area economy just as effectively as if it were in greenbacks issued by the U.S. Treasury with James Madison's picture on each "frogskin." It's money.

The process is called *monetization* of a declared value, converting that static underused asset into *money*. Here are large scale examples of monetizing underused assets—i.e. declared or undeclared values:

• Hitler's issuance of German marks against the production of goods and services, and war machines, during the fascist regime, 1938-1945. Also, granting of massive wartime credits (loans) to German companies.

• Loans of $500 and $800 per acre to Wenatchee and Yakima apple growers for expansion in the 1920s, which laid the basis for their bankruptcy in the 1930s. The declared equity in their farm properties proved to be fallacious.

• Ronald Reagan's national debt expansion of $2.5 trillion in our decade of the 1980s, accompanied by issuances of $10 trillion of private credit, all monetized and spent. Who will pay and when?

• The issuance of low interest loans to private borrowers by the Japanese government against steeply rising values of urban real estate (land), which *created* multi-trillion funds for use by Japanese corporations for domestic and world investments and expansion, including buying many U.S. banks, companies, the Rockefeller Center—and the lucrative U.S. automobile and electronic markets.

All of these are examples of monetizing *transient* values, kinds that are subject to wide fluctuations or evaporating entirely, as demonstrated in the Savings & Loan financial debacle. Will Japan's credit system collapse, too? Who among you, the readers of this brief essay, is free of the gnawing thought: "With the burden of nearly $14 trillion public and private debt, how can the U.S. financial system possibly avoid a cataclysmic depression, a wipe-out of the bloated values of our land, houses, farms and businesses?"

Who, ultimately, pays the inter-laced network of loans and obligations, following an unchecked monetizing process, such as the one ignited by the Reagan presidency or the one currently happening in Japan?

The record shows the books are wiped clean, nearly clean, by the cleansing procedures of default, bankruptcy debt adjustment and remonetizing at an amazing low level of realistic market values.

I participated as a young agricultural financial officer in that previous depression process, and I believe I am equipped to provide glimpses of what happened. First, let's describe the scenario.

• Captive of a non-competent Congress and financial system, the Hoover administration drank bitter dregs of defeat in 1932. The nation's banking system had collapsed. Fifteen million urban Americans were unemployed. A million farmers (out of six million) were on relief. Driven by depression and drought, two million midwest and southcentral farm and rural families fled west into Oregon, Washington, Idaho and California, seeking new farms, jobs and business bases.

• The demands for effective public action under bold national leaders were imperative. Franklin Roosevelt, a basically nonqualified man of good spirit, knew this and accepted structured, disciplined counseling from Rexford Guy Tugwell,

Professor George Warren, Harold Ickes, Henry Wallace, Paul Appleby and others. Walter Lippman said, "The only real qualification this man has is that he so eagerly wants to be president." Franklin Roosevelt was a *psychological* leader. The new 1932 Congress was willing to be led.

With those new national assets—a civic/responsible Congress and an articulate, well-counseled President—our country built the engines for overhauling the farm and rural economy, commencing with massive debt adjustment and remonetization of land values at functional (depression) levels. These were the key Public Laws and Executive Orders promulgated to handle the essential tasks:

An Executive Order (by the President) created the Resettlement Administration in April 1935. Under this authority, the Resettlement Administration could:

• Buy large tracts of good farm land, reappraise it, wipe out excess value, subdivide it into functional family type farms, improve it with homes and farmsteads and sell or lease the new farms to qualified settlers, including midwest migrants.

• Make rehabilitation loans to non-bankable (bankrupt) farm families, after adjusting (wiping out) excess debts, and on the basis of viable new farm and family plans. This, also, was a remonetization process, as explained below.

• Make cooperative loans and grants, in order to equip qualified non-bankable farmers with up-to-date farm machinery, breeding stock, water systems, seed stocks and new technology at affordable costs.

The Bankhead-Jones Farm Tenant Act of 1937 was passed by Congress following the President's Emergency Order. It achieved the following:

• Created the Farm Security Administration to continue and extend the "supervised credit" system launched by the Resettlement Administration, making loans and grants to non-bankable farm families.

• Took over the authorized tasks of the Resettlement Administration in resettling and serving displaced (migrant) farm families.

• Developed and administered the cooperative loan component of rural community rehabilitation.

• Authorized the Farm Tenant Purchase Program to assist and finance tenants in purchasing their rented farms at reappraised and viable values. Made real estate loans for these purposes.

All of these financial and remedial services properly served the country's rural economy, which had been shattered by the forces of the Great Depression which, in turn, was spawned by irresponsible, uncontrolled monetization of spurious land and commercial values during 1920-1930.

These features are of interest to both historians and prescient people looking ahead toward our future needs:

• In 1935-1936, while our banking and credit system was badly damaged, Congressional appropriations were the main sources of money for monetary infusions to finance imperative public agency services, and to avoid violent revolution in the United States. Congress *created* the money.

• Later, as we restored vitality in the national financial system, our government "bought" the money for these emergency and remedial programs and services in the New York money markets at average costs of 1 1/2%. In turn, we loaned the money to farmers for real estate loans at 3% on 40 year amortization agreements. The annual payments for interest and principal were 4.326%, or about $650 per year for a typical family type farm.

• It follows that this debt adjustment and remonetization process was based, for its vitality and success, on a very low cost of money and interest rate.

• Under provisions of the "supervised credit system," we *monetized*, in unorthodox fashion, in order to serve the needs of bankrupt families:

1. The integrity and work skills of the family.
2. A viable improved farm *and family* business plan.
3. Infusion of improved technology into the farming opera-

tion, so it could generate sufficient income to pay adjusted obligations (debts).

• We utilized sound guides and procedures for reappraising farm land and property in order to create a viable basis for debt adjustment and remonetization; i.e., making new real estate loans. In this procedure, we determined "long term" value and the "earning capacity" of the farm, using these depression level factors and criteria:

1. We forecast the farm (wholesale) prices of the main farm crops and products; for example, $1.50 per bushel for wheat, 5 cents per pound for hogs, 7 cents per pound for beef and 30 cents per pound for butterfat (cream). Thus, we projected realistic values for farm crop sales.

2. We forecast average yields of crops and products under the prevalent climate, management and other conditions.

3. We forecast sales and income per acre and for the entire farm; thereupon, determined (capitalized at 3%) land and farm values.

4. On the basis of these guides, we adjusted debts and determined repayable levels for new loans. Recently for purposes of this introduction, I consulted with able people in the History Section of USDA's Economic Research Service. Together, we decided that the financial and rural rehabilitation services described above, during 1935-1941, were conducted with a total of about $2 billion of loans, grants and field services.

I participated in certain assessments of this innovative financial service and studied repayment records, comparing performance of these bankrupt farmers with the performance of "credit-worthy" farmers who borrowed from commercial banks in the same depression era. The evidence shows that the bankrupt group achieved the better aggregate payment record. The supervised credit system is viable. It can be used successfully "monetizing" bankrupt farmers, cleaning up the garbage and debris of uncontrolled inflationary monetizing of spurious values—for example, in the United States S&L debacle, and in Japan's dizzy ascent which precedes its fall, sure as evening follows daytime.

About one hundred ten years ago, Henry George published *Progress & Poverty* in which he explained the phenomenon of land value inflation and seriously proposed the "single tax," i.e., a tax to recover "unearned increment" when urbanization enhances the value of land without investments or improvements by the owner.

Henry George said, "The value of a piece of land is determined by the number of people who pass by the front gate each day."

He said, "Since growth of the community creates this unearned increment in value, it is right and proper that the community should tax and recover it, or a large share of it, for use paying for road, school and other civic services." These were his observations and proposals one hundred ten years ago, before America unleashed its rampant urbanization process, progressively since 1950.

Today, America has a gridlock at its front gate. Japan has an aggravated civic/financial disease.

Today, Japan can buy the Empire State Building, half of California's banks and 70% of America's automobile market. Tomorrow, a dread financial disease will decimate the massed humanity at the Empire State building's front gate. The massive unearned value will evaporate like morning mist. It was a bad investment, Asian friends.

The guy who said, "There are no free lunches," just came by. This time he said "Don't count your value until you can eat it."

And he said, "You can monetize fallacious value only once per boom and bust cycle. There ain't no next time."

And he said, updating Henry George, "When too many damned people get in front of your front gate, it's hell living there anymore."

I am getting ready to dust off my Big Depression uniform. It was fun wearing it then, working for our pleasant only-fairly-competent President Franklin Roosevelt. Maybe this time it will be fun again.

INDEX

INDEX